# LABORATORY Manual

# BIOLOGY

## CBSE Class XII

*Author*
Samiksha Gupta

**Name**..........................................................................................................

**Class**.......................... **Section**.......................... **Roll No**..........................

**School**.........................................................................................................

**Arihant Prakashan** (School Division Series)

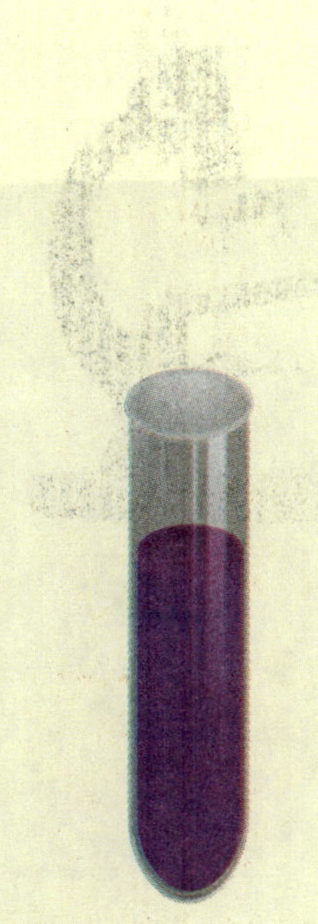

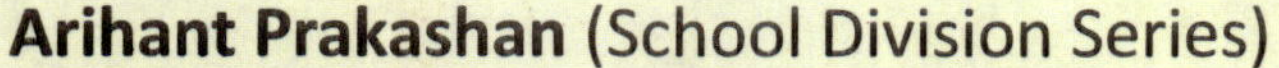

**Arihant Prakashan** (School Division Series)

## Administrative & Production Offices

**Regd. Office**
'Ramchhaya' 4577/15, Agarwal Road, Darya Ganj, New Delhi -110002
Tele: 011- 47630600, 43518550; Fax: 011- 23280316

**Head Office**
Kalindi, TP Nagar, Meerut (UP) - 250002, Tel: 0121-7156203, 7156204

## Sales & Support Offices

Agra, Ahmedabad, Bengaluru, Bareilly, Chennai, Delhi, Guwahati, Hyderabad, Jaipur, Jhansi, Kolkata, Lucknow, Nagpur & Pune

**Price :** ₹350.00

**PO No. :** TXT-59-T071730-7-26

Published by Arihant Publications (India) Ltd.

For further information about the books from Arihant, log on to **www.arihantbooks.com** or email to **info@arihantbooks.com**

Follow us on   

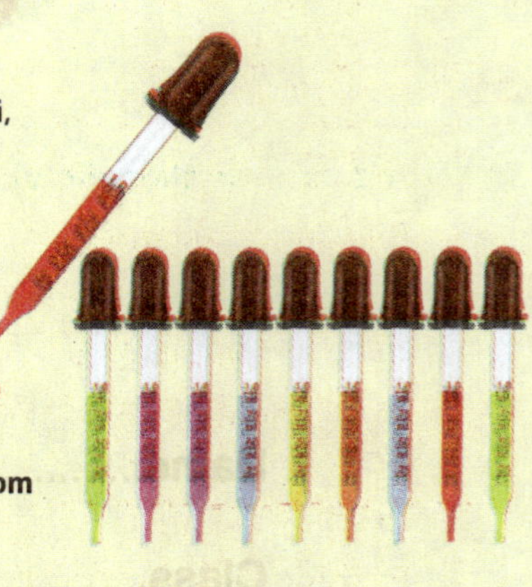

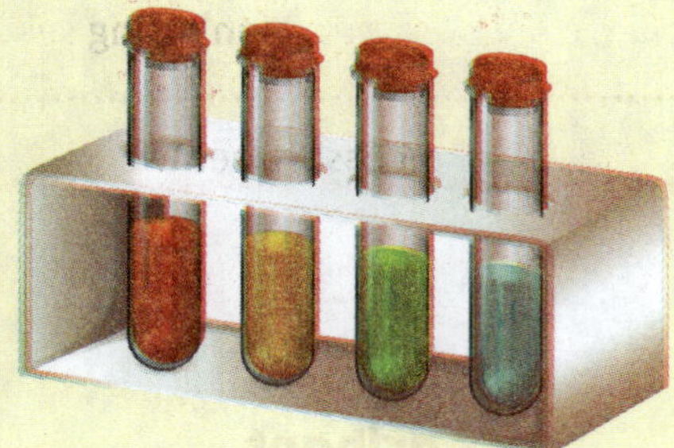

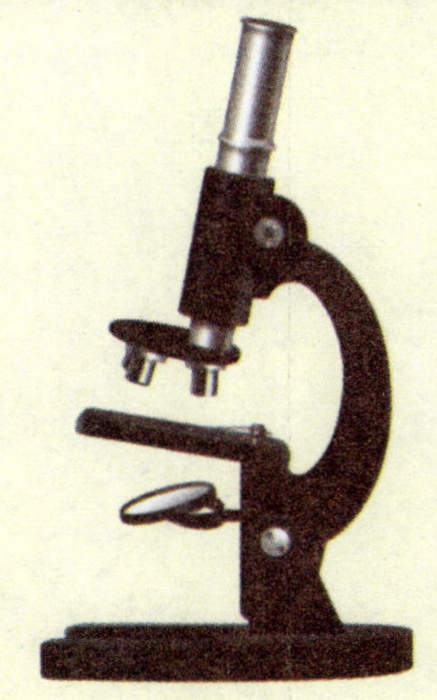

# Contents

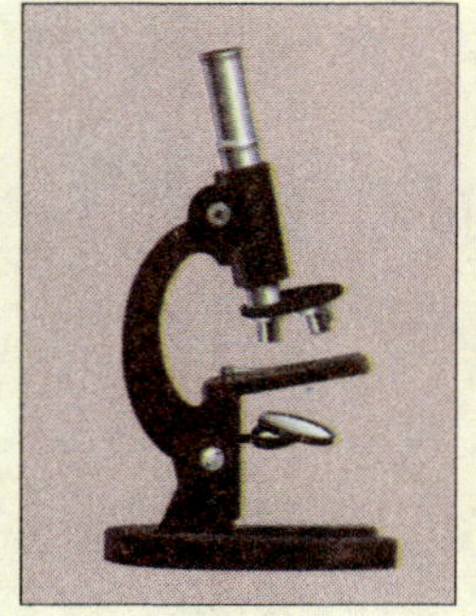
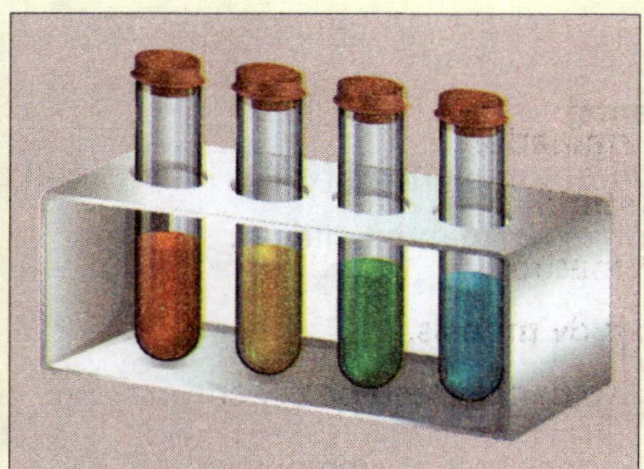

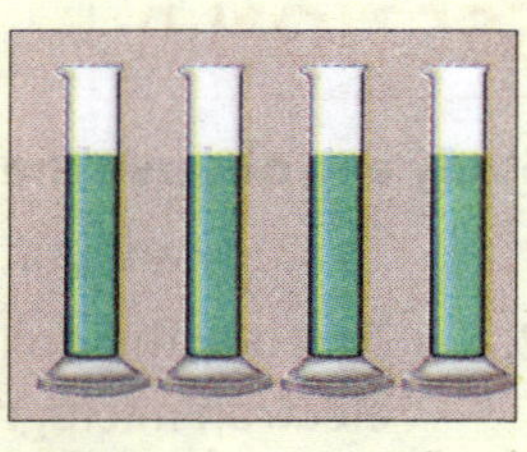

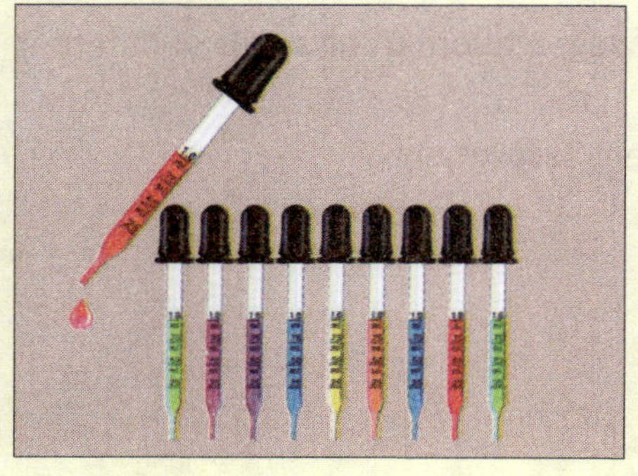
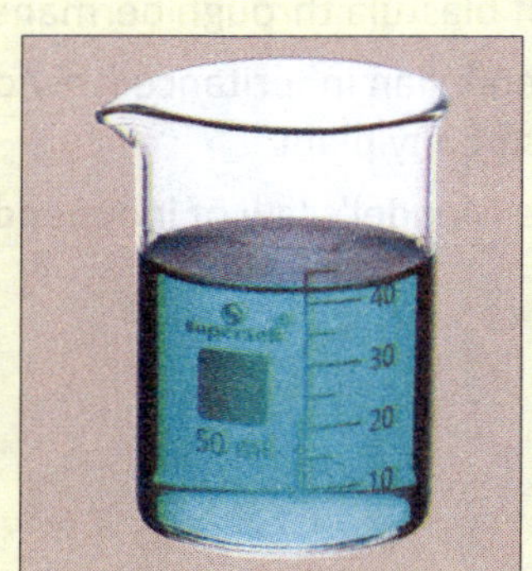

40
30
20
50 ml
10

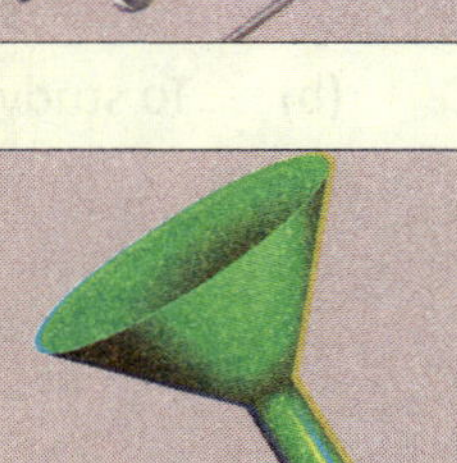

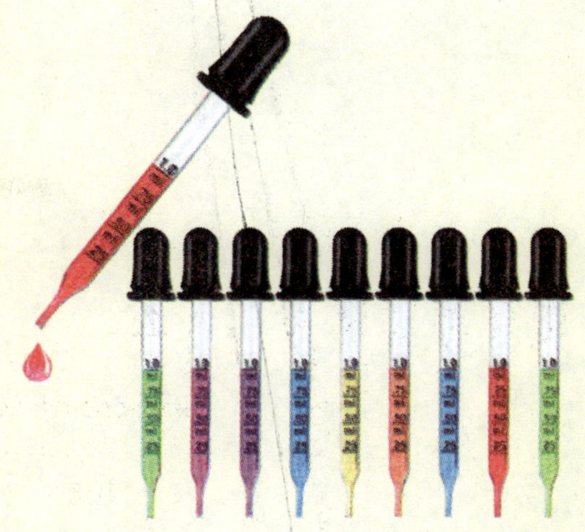

| Time allowed : 3 Hours | | Max. Marks : 30 |
|---|---|---|
| **Evaluation Scheme** | | **Marks** |
| One Major Experiment 5 | | 5 |
| One Minor Experiment 2 & 3 | | 4 |
| Slide Preparation 1 & 4 | | 5 |
| Spotting | | 7 |
| Practical Record + Viva Voce | (Credit to the student's work over the academic session may be given) | 4 |
| Investigatory Project and its Project Record + Viva Voce | | 5 |
| Total | | 30 |

## SECTION A

### List of Experiments

1. Prepare a temporary mount to observe pollen germination.
2. Study the plant population density by quadrat method.
3. Study the plant population frequency by quadrat method.
4. Prepare a temporary mount of onion root tip to study mitosis.
5. Isolate DNA from available plant material such as spinach, green pea seeds, papaya, etc.

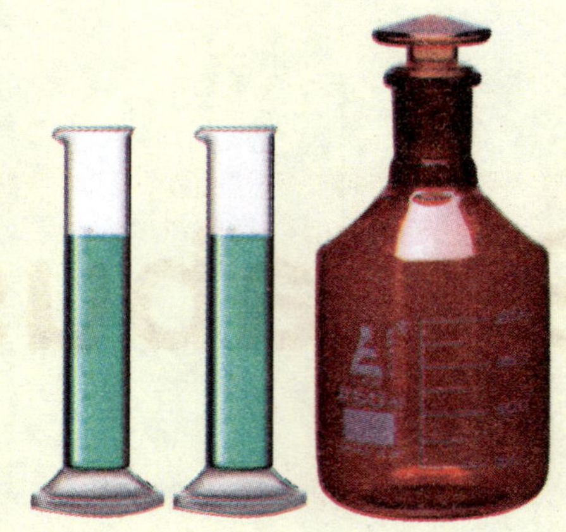

## SECTION B

**Study and observe the following (Spotting)**

1. Flowers adapted to pollination by different agencies (wind, insects, birds).
2. Pollen germination on stigma through a permanent slide or scanning electron micrograph.
3. Identification of stages of gamete development, i.e. T.S. of testis and T.S. of ovary through permanent slides (from grasshopper/mice).
4. Meiosis in onion bud cell or grasshopper testis through permanent slides.
5. T.S. of blastula through permanent slides (Mammalian).
6. Mendelian inheritance using seeds of different colour/sizes of any plant.
7. Prepared pedigree charts of any one of the genetic traits such as rolling of tongue, blood groups, ear lobes, widow's peak and colour blindness.
8. Controlled pollination - emasculation, tagging and bagging.
9. Common disease causing organisms like *Ascaris, Entamoeba, Plasmodium,* any fungus causing ringworm through permanent slides, models or virtual images or specimens. Comment on symptoms of diseases that they cause.
10. Models specimen showing symbolic association in root nodules of leguminous plants, *Cuscuta* on host, lichens.
11. Flash cards models showing examples of homologous and analogous organs.

# INDEX

| S.No. | Name of the Experiment | Page No. | Date | Remarks |
|---|---|---|---|---|

| S.No. | Name of the Experiment | Page No. | Date | Remarks |
|---|---|---|---|---|
| | | | | |

| S.No. | Name of the Experiment | Page No. | Date | Remarks |
|---|---|---|---|---|
| | | | | |
| | | | | |
| | | | | |
| | | | | |
| | | | | |
| | | | | |
| | | | | |
| | | | | |
| | | | | |
| | | | | |
| | | | | |
| | | | | |
| | | | | |
| | | | | |
| | | | | |
| | | | | |
| | | | | |
| | | | | |
| | | | | |
| | | | | |
| | | | | |
| | | | | |
| | | | | |
| | | | | |
| | | | | |
| | | | | |
| | | | | |
| | | | | |
| | | | | |

# INDEX

| S.No. | Name of the Experiment | Page No. | Date | Remarks |
|---|---|---|---|---|
| | | | | |
| | | | | |
| | | | | |
| | | | | |
| | | | | |
| | | | | |
| | | | | |
| | | | | |
| | | | | |
| | | | | |
| | | | | |
| | | | | |
| | | | | |
| | | | | |
| | | | | |
| | | | | |
| | | | | |
| | | | | |
| | | | | |
| | | | | |
| | | | | |
| | | | | |
| | | | | |
| | | | | |
| | | | | |
| | | | | |
| | | | | |
| | | | | |
| | | | | |

LABORATORY Manual

# BIOLOGY

# CERTIFICATE

This is to certify that Experiments recorded in this Practical Notebook have been performed

by ______________________________________
(Student's Name)

of __________ of ______________________________
(Class/Section) (School Name)

during academic session ____________________

| ........................ | ........................ | ........................ |
|---|---|---|
| Examiner Signature | Principal Signature (with school stamp) | Teacher Signature |

# Your Laboratory

A biology laboratory is essential for testing ideas and concepts through experiments because it allows student to directly engage with the biological phenomenon.

It provides a unique learning environment where students develop scientific temper, acquire relevant skills and become familiar with various techniques and methodologies of scientific investigation.

A science student can not truly learn without a laboratory. Learners get exposure to various advanced techniques and tools used in research, preparing them for future endeavours.

## Lab Essentials

To perform experiments successfully, a learner needs to enter the biology laboratory well prepared with following essentials:

1. **A Laboratory Record Book** For documenting all the information including data recordings and their interpretations.
2. **A Laboratory Manual** For detailing the experiments and procedures to be followed.
3. **Dissection Box** Required for various tasks such as handling and manipulating living materials, conducting experiments and preparing slides. It includes scissors, scalpels, forceps, dissecting needles, razor, hand lens, dropper, fine brush, etc.
4. **Laboratory Coat** Required to protect the learner against chemical spills and biological contaminants, ensuring safety and hygiene during experiments.
5. **A Hand Towel** For cleanliness and drying hands.

## Precautions While Working in the Laboratory

- Carefully listen to the teacher's instruction before performing an experiment.
- Be careful while handling sharp tools like scissors, needles, scalpel, razors and forceps.
- Always follow the safety guidelines written on the instruments and chemical containers.
- Be aware of how to use first-aid kit in case someone gets hurt.

# Introduction to Lab Instruments

On routine basis, biological experiments requires the use of some basic equipments. Some of these equipments are discussed in this section.

## Microscope

Microscope is a widely and extensively used instrument found in all biology labs. It magnifies and resolves the object when seen through it. Microscopes of different powers are used to observe microscopic details of any given sample. Microscope works on the basis of two functions:

- **Magnification** It is refer to how many times larger an object appears when viewed through the microscope compared to its actual size.
- **Resolution** The ability of microscope to distinguish two close points as separate entities.

Microscopes are of two types:

(i) **Light Microscope**

It uses light as a source of illumination. It is of two types:

(a) Dissecting microscope

(b) Compound microscope

(ii) **Electron Microscope**

It uses electrons as a source of illumination for the microscopic field.

### a. Dissecting Microscope

It is designed to provide three-dimensional view of objects like insects, plants or larger biological specimens. It is also used to perform dissections of small organisms.

#### Working

- The object or slide with specimen is placed on the stage of the microscope.
- Lens is moved above the slide with the help of a folded arm.
- Adjustment screws are used in order to move the vertical limb to focus on the slide.

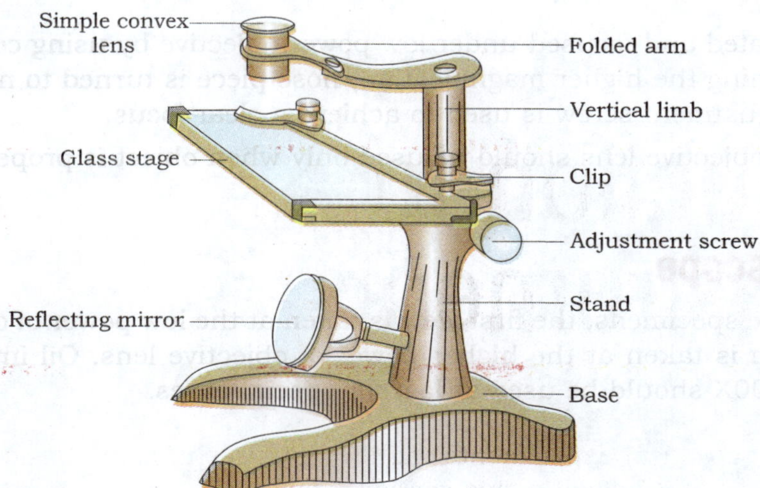


A dissecting microscope

## b. Compound Microscope

It is an optical instrument that uses multiple lenses for the magnification of small objects for detailed observations.

### Working

- The mirror is adjusted in diffused source of light so that sufficient light enters into the microscope.
- The light entering into microscope should be regulated with the help of diaphragm.
- A clean prepared slide is placed on the centre of the stage such that it lies just under the objective lens and is completely illuminated by diaphragm.

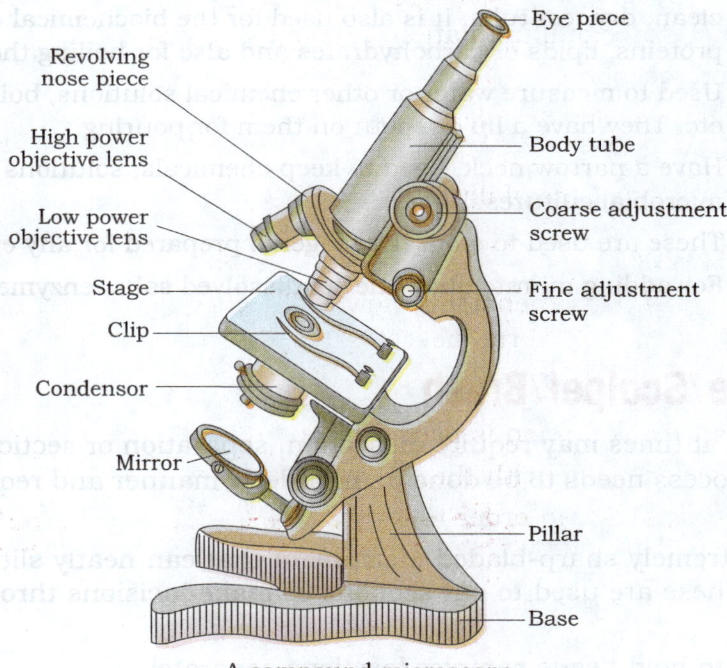


A compound microscope

- The object is located and focused under low power objective by using coarse adjustment screw. For obtaining the higher magnification, nose piece is turned to next higher power lens and fine adjustment screw is used to achieve a clear focus.
- The high power objective lens should be used only when object is properly mounted under coverslip.

## Use of Microscope

While observing the specimens, the first view is taken at the low power of objective lens and the second observation is taken at the higher power of objective lens. Oil immersion lens having magnification of 100X should be used at last for special cases.

## Glasswares

The commonly used glasswares include slides, test tubes, petridishes, beakers, flasks, reagent bottles, funnel, etc.

| | |
|---|---|
| **Slides** | To view a sample under microscope, a specimen is placed on to a clean glass slide. The sample can be fixed or stained on the slide for undisturbed and clear observation. |
| **Coverslips** | Used to cover the section or tissues on the glass slide. |
| **Petridishes** | Used to culture the samples (generally microorganism) by placing them on a nutrient agar or broth medium. |
| **Watch glass** | Used to keep the fine cut sections in water while preparing the slide. Also used for staining the sections. |
| **Test tube** | A sample when requires mixing, addition of solutions, etc. is placed in a clean, dry test tube. It is also used for the biochemical experiments of proteins, lipids or carbohydrates and also for boiling the leaves or tissues. |
| **Beakers** | Used to measure water or other chemical solutions, boil or mix the solutions, etc. They have a lip or spout on them for pouring. |
| **Flasks** | Have a narrow neck, used to keep chemicals, solutions or nutrient media for microbial cultures. |
| **Reagent bottles** | These are used to store the reagents prepared for any experiment. |
| **Glass pipettes** | For adding minute quantities of dissolved salts, enzymes or other solutions. |

## Forceps/Needle/Scalpel/Brush

Biology experiments at times may require dissection, separation or section cutting of animal or plant tissue. This process needs to be done in an orderly manner and requires the use of sharp instruments.

- A **scalpel** is an extremely sharp-bladed instrument that can neatly slit the skin open or cut through tissues. These are used to cut sections or make incisions through muscle and organs.
- **Forceps** are used to hold tissue samples/sections separately.
- **Brush** is used for transferring the sections of specimen from one slide to another slide.

# Apparatus and Glasswares Required in Biology Laboratory

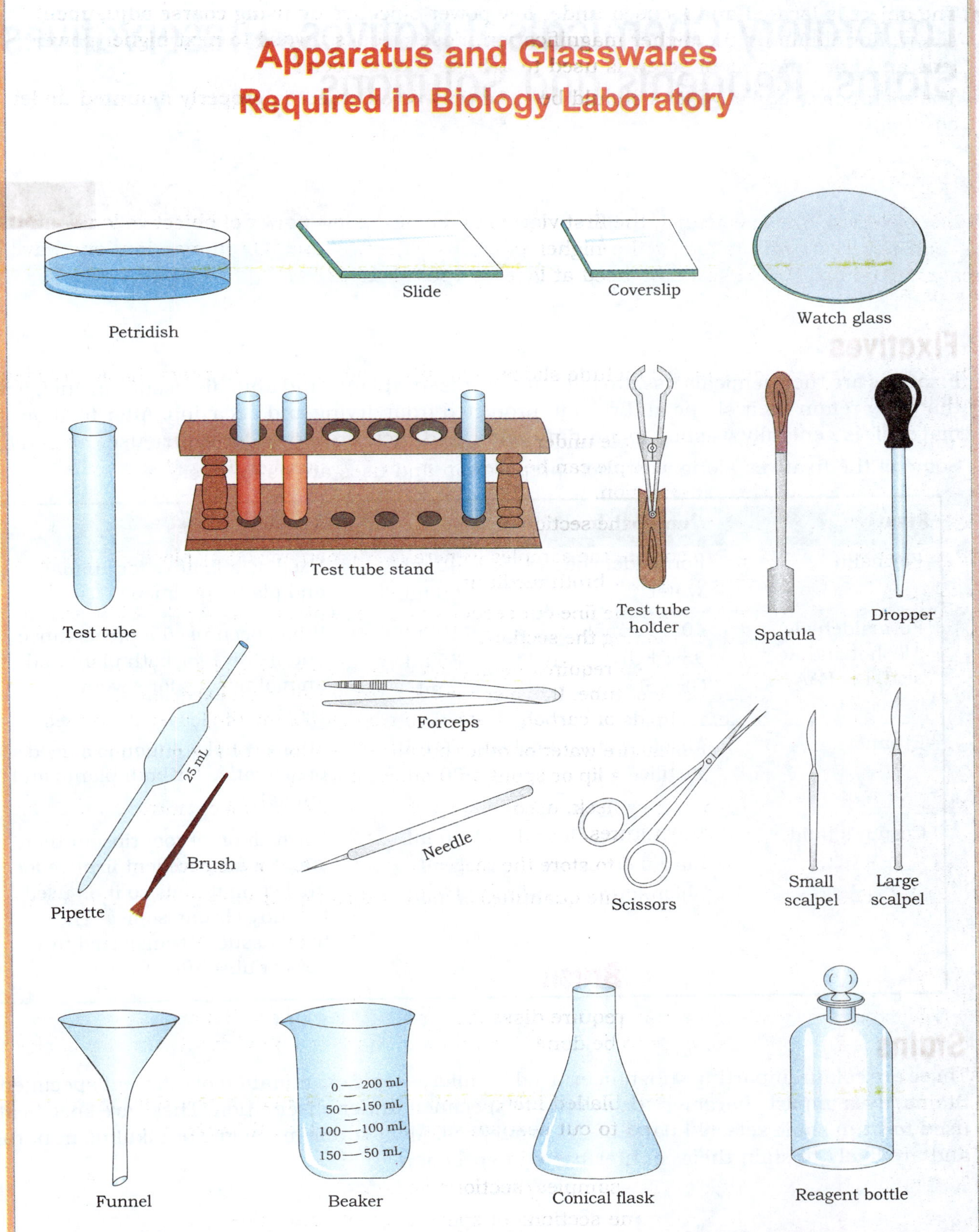

# Laboratory Chemicals, Fixatives, Preservatives, Stains, Reagents and Solutions

## Fixatives

Fixatives are the chemicals used to kill cells or preserve plants and animals tissues in such a way that they retain their shape and remain protected from drying and decaying. After fixation, the material, is generally washed in running water and then preserved for future use.

Some of the fixatives along with their preparation and uses are as follows:

| Fixative | Composition | | Uses |
|---|---|---|---|
| Formalin | Formaldehyde<br>Water | 40 mL<br>60 mL | Used as a fixative for animal and plant specimens. |
| Formaldehyde, Alcohol and Acetic acid, i.e. FAA | 40% Formalin<br>95% Ethyl alcohol<br>Glacial acetic acid | 10 mL<br>85 mL<br>5 mL | It has been used a preservative and fixative for both plant and animal tissues for several years. |
| Ethanol | Absolute ethyl alcohol<br>Distilled water | 70 mL<br>30 mL | 70% alcohol solution is a good preservative for both plants and animals. |
| Carnoy's fluid | 100% Ethyl alcohol<br>Glacial acetic acid<br>Chloroform | 30 mL<br>5 mL<br>15 mL | For fixation of root tips, anther, etc. It is an excellent fixative for nuclear materials so it is used to study chromosomes. The fixed tissue is transferred to 95% or absolute alcohol. |

## Stains

These are colour imparting substances used for microscopic examination of different specimens. Stains/dyes impart characteristic colours to specimen under observation. These are specifically used to stain some selected parts of the tissue/cell. Most stains are acidic or alkaline in nature and are likely to stain their counter parts in specimen.

The most commonly used stains in biology laboratory are discussed below:

| Stains | Composition and Preparation | | Uses |
|---|---|---|---|
| 1. **Acetocarmine** | Carmine powder | – 1 g | Stains chromosomes dark red. Commonly used to study chromosomes during cell division. |
| | Glacial acetic acid | – 45 mL | |
| | Distilled water | – 55 mL | |
| | Ferric acetate | – A few drops | |
| | Dissolve carmine powder in the mixture of acetic acid and water by boiling. Add a few drops of ferric acetate on cooling. Filter and store the solution in a dark bottle. | | |
| 2. **Safranin** | Safranin powder | – 1 g | Used to stain lignified tissues, cutinised tissues and nucleus. |
| | Ethyl alcohol (50%) | – 100 mL | |
| | Dissolve safranin powder to the alcohol and store the solution in a clean bottle. | | |
| 3. **Methylene blue** (Wright's blood stain) | Methylene blue | – 0.9 g | Used for staining blood tissue specimen. |
| | Sodium bicarbonate | – 0.5 g | |
| | Distilled water | – 95 mL | |
| | Dissolve sodium bicarbonate in distilled water and add methylene. Boil for one hour then cool, filter and store. | | |
| 4. **Haematoxylin** | Haematoxylin | – 4 g | Used as a nuclear stain. |
| | Ethyl alcohol | – 25 mL | |
| | Saturated aqueous solution of ammonium alum | – 400 mL | |
| | Methyl alcohol | – 100 mL | |
| | Glycerine | – 10 mL | |
| | Dissolve haematoxylin in ethyl alcohol. To this, add saturated aqueous solution of ammonium alum. Expose the solution to light for 48 hours. After this interval, add methyl alcohol and glycerine. Mix these well and keep the solution for 2 months for ripening. Filter and store in stoppered bottles for future use. | | |
| 5. **Iodine stain** (Lugol's) | Potassium iodide | – 10 g | Used for staining flagella, cilia and nuclei of the cells. |
| | Iodine | – 5 g | |
| | Distilled water | – 100 mL | |
| | Dissolve potassium iodide in water followed by addition of iodine to the solution while stirring it continuously. | | |

| Stains | Composition and Preparation | Uses |
|---|---|---|
| 6. **Eosin** (Aqueous) | a. **Aqueous eosin**<br>Eosin powder – 1 g<br>Distilled water – 100 mL<br>Dissolve eosin powder to the distilled water and store it in clean bottle.<br>b. **Alcoholic eosin**<br>Eosin powder – 1 g<br>Ethyl alcohol – 100 mL | Used as a cytoplasmic stain. |
| 7. **Crystal violet** | Crystal violet – 14 g<br>Ethyl alcohol (95%) – 100 mL<br>Dissolve the crystal violet stain in ethyl alcohol and leave it for 2-3 days. Filter and store. | Used to stain bacteria and protozoan. |
| 8. **Basic Fuchsin** | Basic fuchsin – 8 g<br>Ethyl alcohol – 100 mL<br>Dissolve the stain in ethyl alcohol by stirring it continuously. Leave it for three days. Filter and store it. | Used to stain bacteria. |
| 9. **Leishman's stain** | Leishman's stain – 0.15 g (powder)<br>Methyl alcohol – 100 mL<br>Dissolve the stain powder in methyl alcohol and leave it for 48 hours. | Used for staining blood smears. It is used to differentiate and identify leucocytes, malarial parasites and *Trypanosoma*. |
| 10. **Borax carmine** | Borax – 4 g<br>Carmine – 3 g<br>Distilled water – 100 mL<br>Ethyl alcohol (75%) – 100 mL<br>Mix borax powder with carmine powder and dissolve the mixture in distilled water. Now add ethyl alcohol to this mixture. Allow the mixture to stand for three to five days and then filter. | It is generally used to stain cell structure such as nuclei and cytoplasm in tissue sections red. |

## Mounting Media

These are the chemicals which protect the cell/tissues from being dehydrated. These can fix the cell/tissues or section either temporarily or permanently. Some mounting media are described below.

| Mounting media | Preparation and composition | Uses |
|---|---|---|
| 1. **Glycerine** | Gelatin – 10 g<br>Distilled water – 60 mL<br>Pure glycerine – 70 mL<br>Phenol crystals – 0.25 g<br>Dissolve gelatin in distilled water by heating it.<br>Add glycerine and phenol while the solution is still hot. | • It is used as a temporary mounting media. |
| 2. **Canada balsam** | Canada balsam – 60 g<br>Xylene – 100 mL<br>Dissolve this balsam in xylene in an oven. | • It is a natural resin from balsam fir tree.<br>• Used for permanent slide fixation. |
| 3. **D.P.X** | Distrene 80 – 10 g<br>Dibutyl phthalate – 5 mL<br>Xylene – 35 mL | • It is most commonly used mountant.<br>• Used for permanent slide preparation. |
| 4. **Lactophenol** | Phenol crystals<br>Lactic acid<br>Glycerine<br>Distilled water<br>Cotton blue (For staining fungi)<br>Mix all the mentioned constituents in equal measure. | • It is used as mounting medium and staining agent for fungi. |

## Biochemical Reagents and Solutions

Some solutions are generally used to test the presence of chemicals in the given samples. The most commonly used biochemical reagents and solutions are listed as follows:

| Reagents/ Solutions | Preparations and composition | Uses |
|---|---|---|
| 1. **Acid water/Acid alcohol** | a. Conc. HCl – 1-2 drops<br>Distilled water – 100 mL<br>b. Conc. HCl – 2 drops<br>70% Alcohol – 100 mL | It is used to remove excess of aqueous or alcoholic stain from the tissues. |

| Reagents/ Solutions | Preparations and composition | Uses |
|---|---|---|
| 2. **Benedict's reagent** | Sodium citrate – 173 g<br>Sodium carbonate (anhydrous) – 100 g<br>Copper sulphate – 17.3 g<br>Distilled water – 1000 mL<br>Dissolve sodium citrate and sodium carbonate in 800 mL water. Dissolve copper sulphate in 100 mL water, mix the two and make it 1000 mL. | • It is used to test the presence of reducing sugars. |
| 3. **Fehling's solution A** | Copper sulphate – 70 g<br>Distilled water – 1000 mL | • It is used to test the presence of reducing sugars. |
| 4. **Fehling's solution B** | Potassium hydroxide – 350 g<br>Potassium sodium tartarate – 350 g<br>Distilled water – 1000 mL<br>***Note*** Fehling's solution A and B should be mixed in equal volumes, only when needed for use. | • It is used to test the presence of reducing sugars. |
| 5. **Biuret reagent** | 3% Copper sulphate – 95 mL<br>10% Potassium hydroxide – 1000 mL | • It is used to test the presence of proteins in biochemical test. |
| 6. **Millon's reagent** | Mercury – 100 g<br>Nitric acid – 200 mL<br>Distilled water – 600 mL<br>Dissolve mercury in nitric acid and dilute it with water.<br>***Note*** Never add water to acid. To dilute the concentrated acid, add acid to water slowly and carefully, to avoid bubbling. | • It is used to test the presence of proteins in biochemical test. |
| 7. **Buffer solution** | a. M/15 $Na_2HPO_4 \cdot 12H_2O$ solution<br>$Na_2HPO_4 \cdot 12H_2O$ – 23.88 g<br>Distilled water – 1 L<br>b. M/15 $KH_2PO_4$ solution<br>$KH_2PO_4$ – 9.08 g<br>Distilled water – 1 L | • These are used to maintain pH within a range. |

# Some Common Procedures and Practices

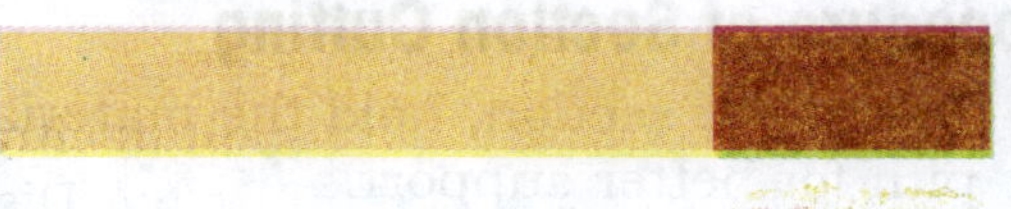

The study of biological parts and processes requires the use of few basic techniques in the laboratory. Some of these skills are mentioned below.

## Peeling

- This method requires the removal of an intact section of leaf epidermis layer.
- Separating out a peel from leaf requires a needle and forceps.
- A small part of sample is broken with care, leaving a thin translucent membrane.
- The peel pulled apart is placed on a slide or watch glass in a drop of water and is then stained or mounted for study.

e.g. To study the structure of stomata, a thin peeled section of leaf is required.

## Smearing

This technique involves the uniform spreading of cells from a section or sample as a single layer over specific area of slide. The cells get smeared during spreading, which permits a clear study of given process.

- The sample is placed in stain and crushed with scalpel or another slide. By doing this, large pieces are removed.
- The second slide is now placed on the corner and run it over the sample using uniform, but gentle pressure.
- The slide is then gently heated over a flame. It is then covered with coverslip after mounting it with appropriate mounting medium and sealed with melted wax or transparent nail polish.

e.g. Root tips of onion, anthers of *Tradescantia*, blood cells of human, etc are widely used for smear preparations.

## Section Cutting

Sections are cut to study the internal structure of an object. It is used for examining the stem, root or leaf. A thin, nearly transparent section is cut with the help of sharp razor or blade in the laboratory.

The section can be cut in two planes

(i) **Transverse Section** (TS) This section passes at a right angle to the longitudinal axis.

(ii) **Longitudinal Section** (LS) This section passes at a right angle to the transverse axis.

Sometime, sections are cut in vertical plane. This is known as Vertical Section (V.S.), e.g. section of leaf.

## Procedure of Section Cutting

- To cut the section, hold the material between your thumb and first finger or embed it in a pith for better support.
- Now, hold the razor in your right hand and cut several thin sections in a single motion.
- Collect the sample immediately in the watch glass containing water, so as to prevent them from drying or destroying.
- Select a suitable section and place it on the slide with the help of brush for further staining and studying.

## Staining

To study the section prepared of plant or animal cells, it is necessary to differentiate them properly. This is achieved by staining the sections using specific stains or dyes.

The stain imparts characteristic colour to different components and helps in distinguishing different tissues, cellular inclusions, etc clearly.

1. **Single Stains** In this, only a single stain is used for the sample to be studied.
   *Example* – Safranin, aniline blue, etc.
   Filaments of algae, fungi, sections of pollens, spores, etc. can be studied using these stains.
2. **Combination of Stains** In this, two or more stains are employed or used to differentiate or distinguish different tissues, cells or cell inclusions. For this purpose, one acidic dye and one basic dye of contrasting colour are generally used. It is used for the sections of stem, root or leaves.
   The several combination of stains used are:
   (i) Hematoxylin (basic stain) and eosin (acidic stain).
   (ii) Safranin (basic stain) and fast green (acidic stain).
   (iii) Safranin (basic stain) and aniline blue (basic stain).
   (iv) Safranin (basic stain) and crystal violet (basic stain).

## Mounting

Mounting is done to protect the section from drying or destroying and to preserve it for longer period of time. Glycerine, DPX or Canada balsam may be used for this purpose.

- When the mounting is done by using glycerine, the slide prepartion is said to be **temporary** while, when mounting is done by using permanent mount like DPX or Canada balsam, the slide preparation is said to be **permanent.**
- Mounting is done by pouring a drop of mounting medium on the section over slide.
- Place a coverslip very gently over it so that no bubble should appear.
- Wipe off the extra mounting medium from the sides of the coverslip with the help of cotton or blotting paper.

- Now, the slide is ready for study.
- In case of permanent slide, prepare a label describing your name and description of material mounted. Fix this label on the glass slide. The description of section (as name of plant and its part) can also be posted on to the slide.

## Drawing the Diagram

Make illustrations using pencil only and it should be drawn on the centre of the page. The image drawn on the paper should be proportionate in size with the actual object or specimen or image. Illustrations should be drawn directly by keeping the object in front and not from the book. All the diagrams or illustrations should be well-labelled. Two lines of labelling should never cross each other. An appropriate caption or heading of the drawing should also be given below it.

## Study of Slides

While studying the slides under the microscope, ensure not to disturb the slide once it is set in appropriate position. Draw the diagrams directly from the slide, not from the book.

## Study of Specimens/Models

Study the characteristics of the specimen from your text book and try to relate your theoretical knowledge with the practical view of the organism (model or specimen). Draw well-labelled diagrams neatly in the record book directly from the actual specimen. Avoid shading and write the comments.

# How to Record An Experiment?

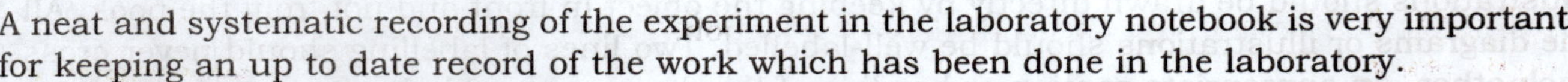

A neat and systematic recording of the experiment in the laboratory notebook is very important for keeping an up to date record of the work which has been done in the laboratory.

Infact, a proper record of the experimental results and conclusions is an indispensable part of scientific work.

The laboratory notebook must be well maintained and protected from mechanical and chemical damage. It should be regularly checked by the teacher.

The experiment should be recorded in the laboratory notebook under the following heads as:

| **Date......** | **Experiment No. ......** | **Page No. ......** |
|---|---|---|

**Aim or Objective of the Experiment** States the overall purpose of the experiment to be performed.

**Theory or Principle** Mention the concept on which the experiment is based in a very brief manner. It also, includes the formula used and clearly explains the symbols involved.

**Apparatus and Materials Required** Mention the name of the apparatus and chemicals to be used in the experiment clearly.

**Procedure** Mention various steps in the experiment to be followed.

**Chemical Reactions** The chemical reactions that take place in the experiment should be written on the left hand side of notebook.

**Diagrams** Wherever required, draw the diagrams on the left hand side of the notebook.

**Observations** Record the observations or data in a tabular format, avoiding any overwriting.

**Calculations** [wherever desirable] For writing the calculations, substitute the observed value in the formula and do the computations systematically and neatly.

**Result** State the conclusions drawn from the experimental observations. If the result depends upon the conditions of temperature and pressure, mention these conditions also along with the result.

**Precautions** Mention the precautions observed during the setup of the apparatus and while performing the experiment.

**Discussion** Under this heading any special inferences or special difficulties faced during the experimentation is been mentioned. These may include points for making the experiment more accurate and for better understanding of the basic principle involved.

SECTION-A

# Experiment 1

## AIM

To prepare a temporary mount to observe pollen germination.

## Theory/Principle

Pollen grains are male reproductive structures of an angiospermic flower that contains male gametes. In nature, pollen grains germinate on compatible stigma of the carpel through **pollen-pistil interaction**. It is an essential step in fertilisation of angiosperms which determines compatibility or incompatibility of both pollen and pistil.

This dynamic process involves pollen recognition, followed by inhibition or promotion of pollen germination. However, the pollen grains can be induced to germinate in a synthetic medium using chemicals which favour pollen germination such as 10% sucrose solution that facilitates rapid growth of pollen tubes.

During germination, intine (inner wall) of pollen grain emerges out as a pollen tube through one of the germ pores in exine (outer wall) and the pollen tube grows into the genetically compatible stigma only. During the growth of pollen tube, if the generative cell has not divided, it will soon divide into two male gametes.

Out of two male gametes carried in the pollen tube, one fuses with the egg cell while the other fuses with polar nuclei. This process is known as **double fertilisation** which is a characteristic feature of all angiosperms. The pollen of different flowers might differ in their germination time and length of the pollen tubes. They also show different **sculpturing** on their pollen wall.

## Requirements

Mature pollens of any seasonal flower like, *Tradescantia*, jasmine, lily, etc. glass slides, coverslips, microscope, distilled water, beaker, weighing machine, glass rod,10mg boric acid, 10g sucrose, 30 mg calcium nitrate, brush and dropper.

## Procedure

1. Firstly, prepare pollen germination medium by dissolving 10g sucrose, 30 mg calcium nitrate and 10 mg boric acid in 100 mL of distilled water in a beaker. Alternatively, 10% sucrose solution can also be used as the medium.
2. Put a drop of this prepared medium or 10% sucrose solution with the help of a dropper on the glass slide.
3. Take a mature flower, break the fresh anther and dust a few pollen grains onto the same glass side.
4. Now, place a coverslip over the prepared slide.

5. Keep the slide containing pollen undisturbed for 10-15 minutes.
6. Carefully observe it under the microscope.

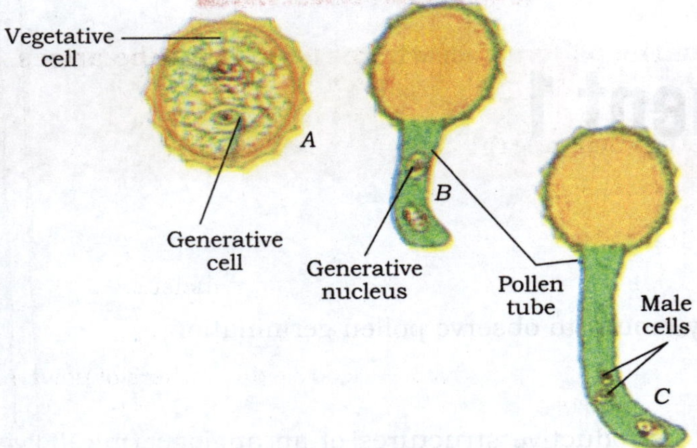


**Fig. 1.1** Stages in the germination of pollen grain

## Observation

1. Some pollen grains will germinate and develop a pollen tube and these are referred to as viable pollen grains.
2. Whereas, other pollen grains that do not germinate and develop a pollen tube are known as non-viable pollen grains.

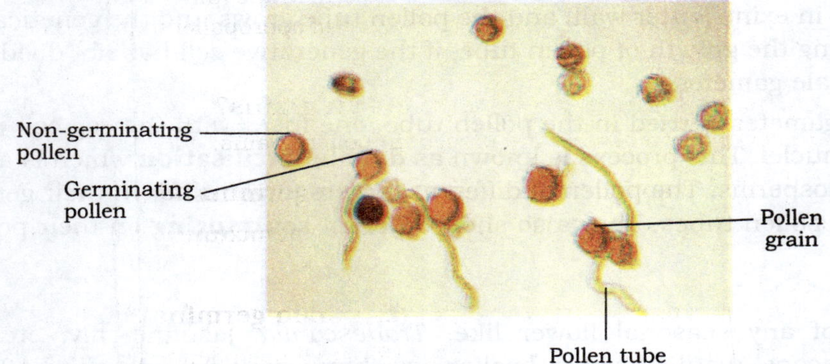


**Fig. 1.2** Pollen germination under microscopic field

## Result

The pollens of different species, in the medium, germinate with different percentage. Also, there is a great variation in time taken for the germination of pollen of each species.

### PRECAUTIONS

- *The nutrient solution should be made carefully otherwise, pollen grains might fail to germinate.*
- *Only few pollen grains should be dusted onto the nutrient solution in order to avoid overcrowding.*
- *While placing coverslip, air bubbles should be avoided else they might interfere with observation and counting of pollens.*
- *The entire process should be carried out at room temperature.*

## Viva-Voce

**Q.1 Name the area of the pollen from where the pollen tube arises.**

**Ans** Germ pores.

**Q.2 How many pollen tubes emerge from a pollen grain?** NCERT

**Ans** Only one pollen tube emerges from a pollen grain.

**Q.3 What does a pollen tube carry?** NCERT

**Ans** Pollen tube carries two male gametes and one vegetative nucleus.

**Q.4 What are pollens?**

**Ans** Pollen consist of the male gametophytes produced by the anthers of flowers or the male cones, essential for plant fertilisation.

**Q.5 Define exine.**

**Ans** Exine is the tough outer layer of a pollen grain or spore that provides protection and aids in identification and dispersal.

**Q.6 Pollen grains shows great variation in their morphology and structure. Name the branch of science which deals with it.**

**Ans** Science which deals with the study of pollen grain is called palynology.

**Q.7 What is the chemical nature of pollen grain walls?**

**Ans** The pollen grain has two walls, i.e. exine (outer wall) and intine (inner wall). Intine is chiefly composed of pectocellulose whereas, exine is made up of sporopollenin (the most resistant biological material known so far).

**Q.8 What is the number of chromosomes in pollen grains?**

**Ans** Haploid ($n$) number of chromosomes are present in pollen grains.

**Q.9 Can you explain why some pollen grains fail to germinate?** NCERT

**Ans** When the pollens are not shed at right stage or the nutrient mixture is not effective, they fail to germinate.

**Q.10 Whey do we use sucrose as the medium for pollen germination?** NCERT

**Ans** The sucrose medium serves as a source of energy for growing pollen tube.

# Experiment 2

## AIM

To study the plant population density by quadrat method.

## Theory/Principle

### Population Density

It represents the numerical strength of a particular species (here plants species) in a community per unit area at a specific time and also indicates the relative importance of each species. The unit area may be small or large, depending upon the size and nature of the plant community being studied.

Population density of a species in an ecosystem varies from place to place. It depends upon various factors such as food and water availability, predation, weather conditions, birth rate, death rate and migration rates. It can be calculated by using the following formula:

$$\textbf{Density } (D) = \frac{\text{Total number of individual (s) of the species in all the sampling units (S)}}{\text{Total number of sampling units studied (Q)}}$$

The value thus, obtained is then expressed as number of individuals per unit area. When the measured unit area is divided by the number of individuals the average area occupied by each individual is obtained.

### Quadrat Method

Quadrats are the sampling units of a known area used for studying the population of a given species. These sampling units must be distinct and must not overlap each other. The quadrats having a square frame with dimensions of 1m X 1m are most commonly used for herbaceous plants. Quadrat method is considered as the most preferable method to calculate population density and percentage frequency of different plant species.

The reliability of quadrat method depends on three key factors.

1. The population within each quadrat must be known.
2. The area of each quadrat must be accurately measured.
3. The quadrat must be the representative of an entire area, which can be ensured through a random sampling method.

## Requirments

Cotton/nylon thread (five meters), 4 nails, a hammer or wooden quadrats of size 1m × 1m, paper and pencil.

## Procedure

1. Select an area having varied vegetation for study.
2. Fix four nails with the help of hammer in the selected area such that the area enclosed by them is a square of 1m X 1m dimension. Make the boundaries of the square by tying thread over the nails.

*Or* You can also use a commercially available ready-made quadrat of size 1m × 1m. Keep it over the area under study.

3. Note down the names of all plant species seen in the quadrat. If the names of the plants are not known, assign alphabets, A, B, C, D, E etc. to them.
4. Count the number of individuals of each plant species present in the quadrat and record the data as shown in the observation table ahead.
5. Now, repeat the steps 1 to 4 to obtain data of nine more quadrats placed randomly at the site of study. Take care that all the regions taken as sample areas should be distinct and non-overlapping.

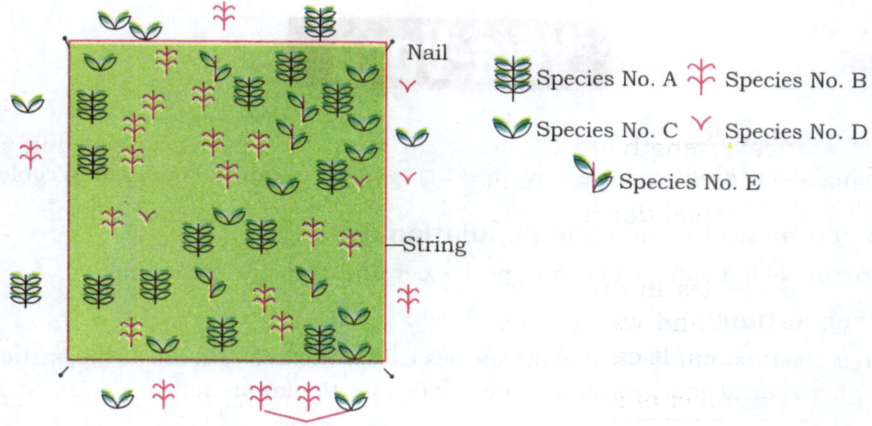


**Fig. 2.1** Occurrence of plant species in a quadrat

**Note** *Suppose you find a new plant variety in any quadrat besides the first, then you must note down the name of the new plant variety and mention 'zero' in all the initially analysed quadrats in which this new variety was absent.*

## Observations

Record your observation in the table given below.

| Plant species | Quadrats employed in study and no. of individuals in each quadrat | | | | | | | | | | Total no. of individuals (S) | Total no. of quadrats studied (Q) | Density (D) $D=\frac{S}{Q}$ |
|---|---|---|---|---|---|---|---|---|---|---|---|---|---|
| | i | ii | iii | iv | v | vi | vii | viii | ix | x | | | |
| A | | | | | | | | | | | | | |
| B | | | | | | | | | | | | | |
| C | | | | | | | | | | | | | |
| D | | | | | | | | | | | | | |
| E | | | | | | | | | | | | | |

## Result/Conclusion

Population density of species will give an idea about the composition of the vegetation. There will be difference in the species composition in the quadrats made in the shady areas, exposed areas with bright sunlight, dry or wet areas, etc.

## PRECAUTIONS

- *The measurement of the quadrats should be accurate.*
- *Count the individuals of one plant species at a time.*
- *Quadrates should be selected from one field only and they should not be very far from each other.*
- *Make sure that the vegetation is not damaged while laying the quadrat.*

# Viva-Voce

**Q.1 What is a quadrat?**

**Ans** Any sampling plot of standard size (say $1m \times 1m$) is called quadrat. It is used in ecological studies.

**Q.2 What do you mean by the term population density?**

**Ans** It is the number of individuals of same species per unit area at a given time.

**Q.3 What is vegetation?**

**Ans** Vegetation is the total numbers of plant species exhibiting different life forms, structure, spatial extent or other special characteristics, specific to a particular area.

**Q.4 Define population.**

**Ans** It refers to the number of individuals of same species that live in a group in a well defined geographical area, share and compete for same resources and can potentially interbreed.

**Q.5 What is community?**

**Ans** An association of different inter-related populations belonging to different species in a common environment which can survive in nature.

**Q.6 Define natality and mortality.**

**Ans** Natality is the birth rate of a species, whereas, mortality is the death rate.

**Q.7 What factors influence the population density?** NCERT

**Ans** Factors such as natality and immigration contribute to an increase in population density, while mortality and emigration contribute to the decrease in population density.

**Q.8 What conclusion can be drawn if density of a plant species is low?** NCERT

**Ans** If the density of a particular species is found low, that indicates the environmental factors are not suitable for that particular species to thrive well.

**Q.9 What is the significance of quadrat method?** NCERT

**Ans**
(i) The quadrat (one metre square) can be randomly drawn with the nail and thread, so we can have a sample quadrat to measure population density anywhere (even at different topography).
(ii) Handling of experiment is easy with this method.

**Q.10 How do plants avoid high plant density in their vicinity?**

**Ans** Plants avoid high plant density in their vicinity by seed dispersal mechanism.

**Q.11 How does the population density of certain plants rapidly increase during monsoon season and decrease in the summer?**

**Ans** The population density of certain plants increases rapidly during the monsoon season due to favourable conditions for growth and reproduction. However, during summer, the population density decreases due to unfavourable conditions that results in high mortality rates among the plants.

# Experiment 3

## AIM

To study plant population frequency by quadrat method.

## Theory/Principle

Population refers to the aggregation of individuals of the same kind inhabitating a particular place or a geographical area at a time.

Frequency is concerned with the degree of uniformity in the occurrence of individuals of a species within a plant community. It is measured by noting the presence of a species in random sample areas (quadrats) which are distributed as widely as possible throughout the area of study. Frequency is the number of sampling units (as %) in which a particular species (A) occurs. The frequency of each species (sps. *A* or sps. *B* or sps. *X*, etc) is expressed in percentage and is calculated as follows:

% Frequency or Frequency index ($F$)

$$= \frac{\text{Number of sampling units (quadrats) in which the species occurs } (N)}{\text{Total number of sampling units (quadrats) employed for the study } (Q)} \times 100$$

## Requirements

Cotton/nylon thread of 5 meters, 4 nails, hammer or wooden quadrat of size 1 m × 1 m, paper and pencil.

## Procedure

1. Select a suitable area, having rich diversity of plants for study.
2. Fix four nails with the help of hammer in the selected area such that the area enclosed by them is a square of 1m × 1m dimension. Make the boundaries of the square by tieing thread over the nails.

   *Or*

   You can also use a commercially available ready made quadrat of size 1 m × 1 m. Keep it over the area under study.
3. List the names of the plant species seen in the quadrat (if the name is not known mark these as species *A* or *B*, etc., and if the same species is seen in other quadrats assign the same alphabet).

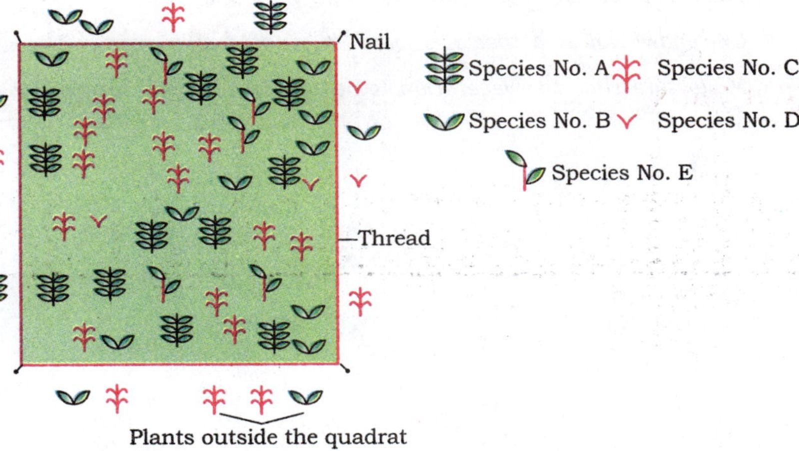


**Fig. 3.1** Occurrence of plant species in a quadrat

4. Similarly, lay nine more quadrats randomly in the field of study.
5. Record the total number of species in ten quadrats and calculate the percentage frequency of occurrence of plants using the formula given.

## Observations

Record your observation in the table given below.

| Plant species | Number of quadrats employed in the study ($Q$) | | | | | | | | | | No. of quadrats in which the species is present ($N$) | Percentage of frequency $F = \frac{N}{Q} \times 100$ |
|---|---|---|---|---|---|---|---|---|---|---|---|---|
| | i | ii | iii | iv | v | vi | vii | viii | ix | x | | |
| *A* | | | | | | | | | | | | |
| *B* | | | | | | | | | | | | |
| *C* | | | | | | | | | | | | |
| *D* | | | | | | | | | | | | |
| *E* | | | | | | | | | | | | |

## Result/Conclusion

Frequency determination using sample areas are often needed to verify general impression about the relative abundance of species. However, frequency alone does not accurately reflect species distribution unless it is correlated with other factors such as density. Typically, when cover and population density are high, the frequency of occurrence of a species will also be high. Plants with a high frequency are often those that are widely distributed.

## PRECAUTIONS

- *The measurement of quadrats should be accurate.*
- *The string or cord used should not be very thick.*
- *One individual of a species should be counted only once in the quadrat.*
- *Make sure that the vegetation is not damaged, while laying the quadrat.*

## Viva-Voce

**Q.1 Define the frequency of a species.**

**Ans** Frequency of a species refers to the percentage of quadrats in which the species present out of the total number of quadrats sampled.

**Q.2 What is the size of the quadrat used in the study?**

**Ans** The size of the quadrat used in the experiment is 1m by 1m.

**Q.3 Define relative frequency of a species.**

**Ans** Relative frequency of a species refers to the frequency of a species per total frequency values for all species.

**Q.4 What is the difference between community and population?**

**Ans** Population is a group of individuals belonging to same species in a given area whereas, community involves number of species living together in a certain environment and interacting with each other.

**Q.5 Define the term 'demography.'**

**Ans** Statistical study of human population is called demography.

**Q.6 If frequency of a plant is high, what will be your interpretation?** NCERT

**Ans** The favourable conditions favour the growth of plants in any area. So, if any species show high frequency in an area, it means all the factors are favourable for the species.

**Q.7 Can many micro-habitat in an area affect frequency of a species? Comment.** NCERT

**Ans** Yes, microhabitats affect the growth, development and survival of a plant, e.g. in a forest, canopy of the plant affect the availability of light to the ground level plants. This variation in light creates different microhabitats, which influence the type of plant species that can grow and thrive in those areas.

**Q.8 Why a quadrat of large size is generally further divided into smaller units?**

**Ans** In smaller units, the individuals of different species can be counted more accurately.

# Experiment 4

## AIM

Prepare a temporary mount of onion root tip to study mitosis.

## Theory/Principle

Somatic growth of both plants and animals takes place by increase in the number of cells. These cells divide mitotically into two daughter cells wherein the number of chromosomes remain unchanged as in the maternal cells. The sequence of events involving cell growth and its division is called **cell cycle**.

Cell cycle consists of four different stages, i.e. $G_1$, S, $G_2$ and M.

1. **$G_1$ or Gap 1 Phase** This is the period of growth phase in which increase in cell mass occurs. Also, the cell prepares itself for DNA synthesis. It is considered to be the longest phase of cell cycle.
2. **S or Synthetic Phase** During this phase, cell continues to grow and synthesise DNA and proteins for M-phase.
3. **$G_2$ or Gap 2 Phase** During this phase, proteins are synthesised in preparation for mitosis while the cell growth continues. $G_1$, S and $G_2$ phases together constitute interphase.
4. **M-Phase** During, this phase, the cell undergoes division, starting with the separation of chromosomes (karyokinesis) and ending with the division of cytoplasm (cytokinesis). Karyokinesis is further divided into four different phases, i.e. prophase, metaphase, anaphase and telophase that results in the division of cell nucleus.

In plants, such divisions takes place rapidly in the meristematic tissues of root and shoot apices, where stages of mitosis can be easily observed. In animals, mitotic cells can be easily observed in the bone marrow tissue of vertebrate, epithelial cells of fish gills and tail of growing tadpole larvae of frog.

## Requirements

Onion bulbs, wide mouthed glass bottle, dropper, blade, forceps, needles, ethyl alcohol, glacial acetic acid, N/10 HCl, 2-4% aceto-carmine or aceto-orcein stain, distilled water, spirit lamp or hot plate compound microscope, slides, blotting paper, coverslips and molten wax/nail polish.

## Procedure

### 1. Growing Onion Root Tips

(i) Select a medium sized onion bulb and carefully remove the dry roots attached to it.

(ii) Place the onion in a wide mouth glass bottle filled with water in such a way that only its base touches the water level.

(iii) Check the water level in the bottle everyday and add few drops of water periodically in order to compensate any evaporation losses.

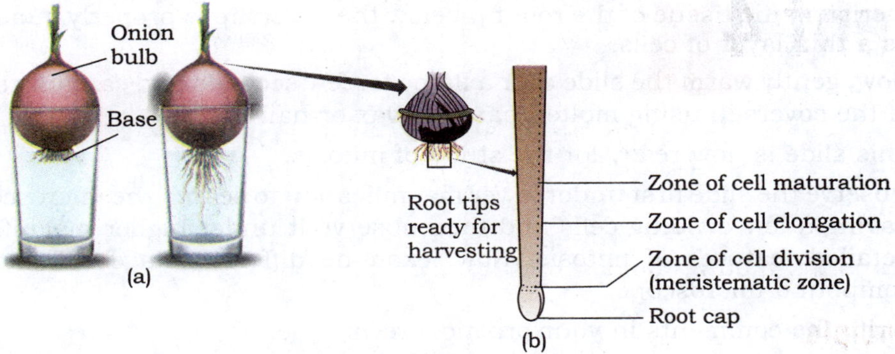


**Fig. 4.1** Method of growing onion roots and different zones of root apex

(iv) Keep them in this position for about 3-6 days as new roots may take that much time to grow.

(v) Cut 2-3 cm long freshly grown roots, 2 hours after the sunrise and keep harvested roots in freshly prepared fixative (glacial acetic acid and ethanol in 1:3 ratio) for 24 hours.

*Note* *As cells onion root tip cell have a cell cycle of 24 hours, i.e. they divide after 24 hours and this division usually takes place about 2 hours after sunrise. Therefore, roots grown on water should be cut only at that time to obtain maximum number of dividing cells.*

(vi) Transfer the roots from fixative to 70% alcohol. Now, these root tips are ideal material for the study of mitotic cell division.

## 2. Preparation and Study of Slide

(i) Take one or two preserved roots using forceps and wash them thoroughly in water on a clean slide.

(ii) Place one drop of N/10 HCl on the root tip followed by 2-3 drops of aceto-carmine or aceto- orcein stain on it using dropper.

(iii) Leave the slide for 5-10 minutes on a hot plate or warm it slightly on a spirit lamp. Care should be taken that the stain is not dried up.

(iv) Blot the excess stain using blotting paper.

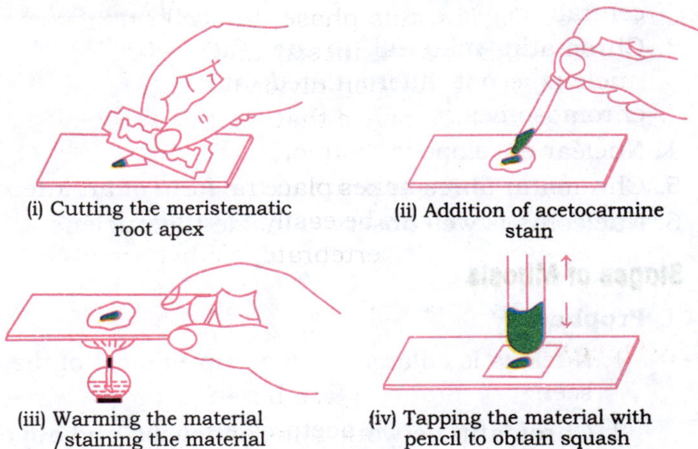


**Fig. 4.2** Preparation of onion root tip squash

(v) Now, cut the comparatively more stained (2-3 mm) tip portion of root using a sharp blade and retain it on slide, discarding the remaining portion.

(vi) After 10-20 seconds, put one or two drops of water and blot them carefully using blotting paper.

(vii) Place the coverslip over the sample and ensure that there are no air bubbles under the coverslip.

(viii) Gently squash the root by tapping the coverslip with the blunt end of a needle so that meristematic tissue of the root tip below the coverslip is properly quashed and spread as a thin layer of cells.

(ix) Now, gently warm the slide over a flame for few seconds and carefully seal the margins of the coverslip using molten paraffin wax or nail polish.

(x) This slide is now ready for the study of mitosis.

(xi) Observe the slide first under lower magnification to search the microscopic field of area having a few dividing cells and then observe it under higher magnification to study detailed features of mitosis. Now, examine different stages of mitosis under the compound microscope.

(xii) Write the comments in your practical record file.

## Observations

Under lower magnification of the microscope, rectangular cells with pink nucleus are seen scattered. Under higher magnification of the microscope, different phases of mitosis become distinct. Those cells which are not in the phases of cell division are considered to be in the interphase. You may observe that most cells in a microscopic field are in interphase.

### Interphase

1. It is a non-dividing phase of the cell cycle occuring between two successive cell divisions.
2. The cells are mostly rectangular, oval or even circular in shape with densely stained nucleus located centrally.
3. Chromatin material inside the nucleus is not differentiated into chromosomes.
4. Nuclear envelope is distinct.
5. Chromatin fibres appears in the form of an interconnected mass within the nucleus.
6. Nucleolus is well observed inside the nucleus.

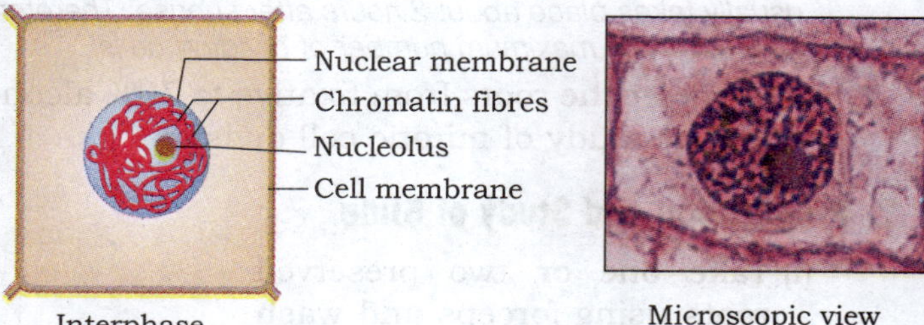


**Fig. 4.3** Interphase stage

### Stages of Mitosis

i. **Prophase**

1. Nucleus is enlarged and occupies most of the cell volume. Intact nuclear outline is also seen.
2. Chromatin network gets condensed and appears as long thread-like structures called chromosomes.

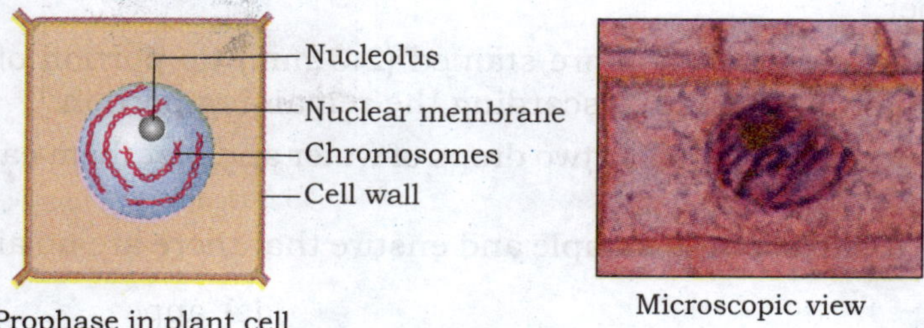


**Fig. 4.4** Prophase stage

3. Nuclear membrane may start disappearing, at the end of prophase.
4. Nucleoli may or may not be visible.
5. If the cell is in early stage of prophase, then the chromatin fibres are very thin. However, in the cells at late prophase, comparatively thicker chromatin fibres would be visible.

ii. **Metaphase**

1. Nuclear membrane disappears completely.
2. Chromosomes become shorter and thicker and hence becomes distinct and clearly visible under the compound microscope.
3. Chromosomes orient themselves along the equatorial plane of the cell, with their centromeres arranged on this plane, forming **metaphase plate**. At this stage, each chromosome consists of two chromatids connected to a region called centromere,which can be seen by changing the microscope resolution.

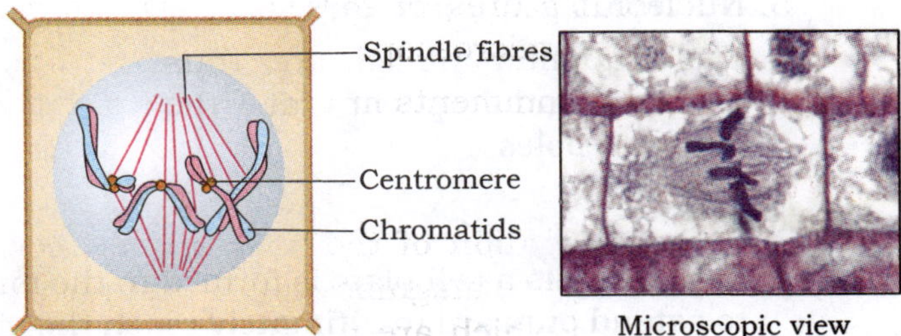


**Fig. 4.5** Metaphase stage

4. Series of spindle fibres attaches the centromeres to the opposite poles.
5. Nucleolus is not observed during metaphase.

iii. **Anaphase**

1. The two sister chromatids of each chromosome separates due to the splitting of centromere and moves towards the opposite poles. Each chromatid is now considered as a distinct chromosome as it possesses its own centromere.

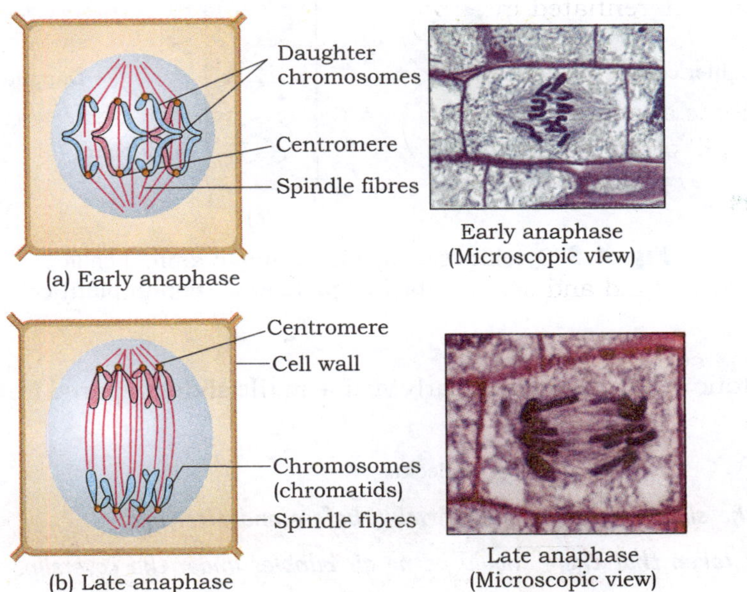


**Fig. 4.6** Anaphase stage

2. The daughter chromosomes (separated chromatids) appears in V, J and I shapes, depending upon the position of the centromere in the chromosomes.
3. Anaphase is designated as early, mid and late stages depending upon the position of moving chromosomes toward the opposite poles.

iv. **Telophase**

1. Chromosomes reach the opposite poles, lose their individuality and look like a mass of chromatin again.
2. Nuclear membrane reappears to form the nuclei of two future daughter cells.
3. Nucleolus gets reappears.
4. Two daughter nuclei are thus formed and appear at the opposite poles.

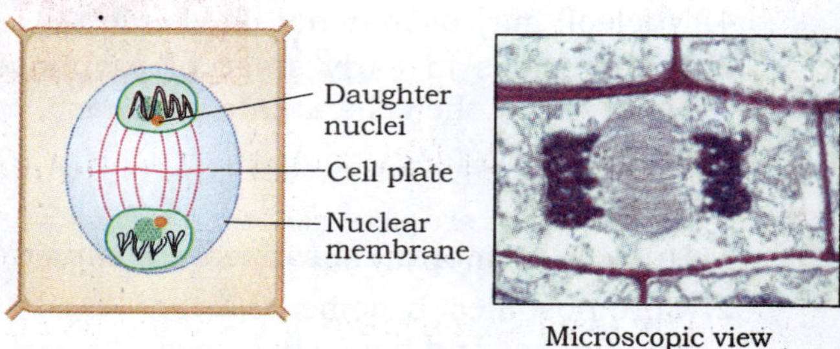


**Fig. 4.7** Telophase stage

## Cytokinesis

1. In plant cells a cell plate is formed in the middle after telophase. The plate can be seen to extend outward to ultimately reach the margin of the cell and divide the cell into two equal halves. Such cell plates are characteristic of plant cells.
2. In animal cell, a furrow appears in the membrane at both sides and grows inward to divide cells into two.

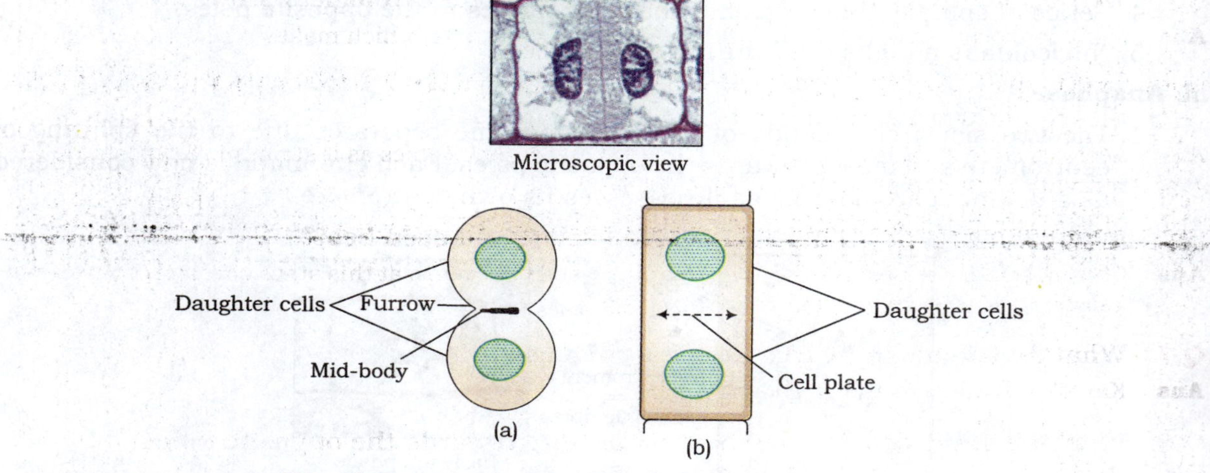


**Fig. 4.8** Cytokinesis: (a) Furrowing in animal cells
(b) Cell plate formation in plant cells

## Result

All the stages of mitotic cell division are clearly visible in the slide prepared from onion root tips.

### PRECAUTIONS

- *Always clean the slide and coverslip thoroughly before and after use.*
- *Care should be taken that there should be no air bubbles under the coverslip.*
- *The base of the onion bulb should exactly be in contact with water, while growing the roots.*
- *The root tip should not dry up during warming.*
- *Material should be mounted on the centre of slide.*
- *The material should only be warmed gently, i.e. do not allow sample to boil on slide while warming.*

## Viva-Voce

**Q.1 Why do we use onion root tips for studying mitosis?**

**Ans** Onion root tips are often used for studying mitosis because these tissues have actively dividing cells and we can easily observe all the stages of mitotic cell divisions in them.

**Q.2 Why is early morning considered as an ideal time to harvest the onion root tips for study of mitosis?**

**Ans** This is because root tips have active cell divisions in early morning. When we cut such material we get all stages of cell division in a single material.

**Q.3 Suggest the name of few tissues, which are suitable for the study of mitosis.** NCERT

**Ans** We can select the dividing cells of

(i) tail of growing tadpole larvae.
(ii) epithelial cells of gills of fishes.
(iii) bone marrow tissue of any vertebrate.
(iv) root tip cells of any herbaceous plant.
(v) shoot apices of plants.
(vi) grasshopper larvae.

**Q.4 Why do we prefer monocotyledonous material for cytological studies?**

**Ans** Many monocots have large, easily observable chromosomes, which makes it easier to study their structure and formation.

**Q.5 Which stain is used for studying chromosomes?**

**Ans** Acetocarmine stain is generally used for studying chromosomes as it stains chromosome deep red while the cytoplasm remains unstained.

**Q.6 In which stage of cell division chromosomes are seen best?**

**Ans** Chromosomes are best seen in the metaphase stage, because at this stage chromosomes are the shortest and exist in the condensed form.

**Q.7 What do you mean by the term 'karyokinesis'?**

**Ans** Karyokinesis means the division of nucleus.

**Q.8 In which stage do chromatids start moving towards the opposite poles?**

**Ans** Anaphase.

**Q.9 Where do spindle fibres attaches on the centromere during cell division?**

**Ans** Spindle fibres attaches themselves on the kinetochores of chromosomes during cell division.

**Q.10 How does cytokinesis differ in animal and plant cells?** NCERT

**Ans** In animals, cytokinesis occurs by cleavage furrow of the cytoplasm, while in plants it occurs by the cell plate method.

**Q.11 State the reason of treating the root tips with $\frac{N}{10}$ HCl.**

**Ans** The HCl soften the tissue making it easier to spread during squashing.

**Q.12 Why is it important to use fixative in mitosis experiment?**

**Ans** Fixatives are important in mitosis experiment because the process of cell division is arrested and the cells can be studied showing different stages of divisions.

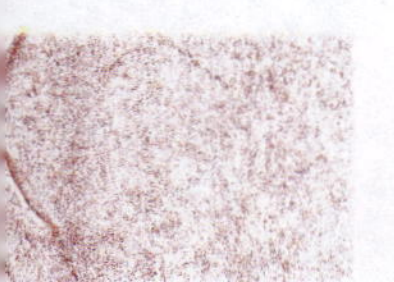

**Q.13 Why mitosis is also known as equational division?** NCER

**Ans** Mitosis is also known as equational division because the number of chromosomes in the daughter cell is equal to the chromosome number in the parent cell.

**Q.14 From where do spindle fibres originate?**

**Ans** Spindle fibres originates from centrioles in case of animal cells, but in plant cells, these originate from the cytoplasm. These are proteinaceous in nature.

**Q.15 Suppose a cell has 44 chromosomes. How many chromosomes will it have after mitosis?**

**Ans** In mitosis, each of the daughter cells produced have the same number of chromosomes (44 chromosomes) as that of the parent cell.

**Q.16 Name the chemical which can inhibit cell division during metaphase stage.**

**Ans** Colchicine is the chemical that inhibits the formation of spindle fibres during metaphase stage.

**Q.17 Name the source of colchicine.**

**Ans** It is obtained from a plant *Colchicum autumnale* belonging to the family–Liliaceae.

**Q.18 What is a phragmoplast?**

**Ans** It is a structure that give rise to cell plate in plant cell during cytokinesis. It is formed in the centre and grows outwardly until it divides the cell into two identical daughter cells completely.

**Q.19 What shape would a metacentric and sub-metacentric chromosome exhibit during the anaphase stage?** NCER

**Ans**

| Types of chromosome | Shape | Centromere position |
|---|---|---|
| Metacentric | *V* | Median |
| Sub-metacentric | *L* | Sub-median |

# Experiment 5

## AIM

To isolate DNA from available plant material like pea seed, spinach, onion, etc

## Theory/Principle

Deoxyribonucleic Acid **(DNA)** and Ribonucleic Acid **(RNA)** are two main types of nucleic acids found in living organisms. DNA serves as the genetic material for most of the organisms. While RNA functions as the genetic material in some **viruses**. Additionally, RNA functions as a messenger, adaptor, structural molecule and in some cases, as a catalytic molecule.

Chemically, DNA is composed of three components, i.e. a pentose sugar (2′ deoxyribose), phosphate group and four types of nitrogenous bases. Majority of the DNA is located in the cell nucleus and the remaining is found in mitochondria and chloroplast.

The process of extraction of DNA from various sources is called DNA isolation. It is a crucial step in gene transfer processes, which can enhance insect resistance, provide protection against viruses, improves herbicide resistance, facilitate storage and enhance protein quality.
The process of DNA isolation consists of three basic steps, as given below

### (i) Homogenisation

This process involves proper grinding or blending of the plant tissue in order to breakdown the cells. For homogenisation, the plant tissue is mixed in a blender with a homogenisation media [including Sodium Dodecyl Sulphate (SDS), Ethylenediamine Tetraacetic Acid (EDTA) and sodium chloride (NaCl). This homogenisation media breaks down the cell wall, cell membrane and nuclear membrane, allowing the release of DNA into the surrounding solution.

### (ii) Deproteinisation

This step involves the addition of a protease enzyme which causes denaturation of proteins. Papain is most commonly used protease enzyme. It eventually denatures the proteins bound to the DNA making the molecule flexible and easy to spool.

### (iii) Spooling

This step involves the precipitation of DNA by adding chilled ethanol (alcohol) which causes every component in the supernatant to stay in the solution except DNA. The DNA gets gathered at the interface of solution which can be then spooled out with the help of a glass rod.

## Requirements

Plant material (like pea-seed, spinach leaves or papaya), mortar and pestle/ blender, muslin cloth, test tubes, enzymes (like cellulase, protease, lipase and ribonuclease), ice-cold 95% ethanol and spool or glass rod.

## Procedure

1. Take small amount of plant material like pea-seed, spinach leaves or papaya and grind it in a mortar with the help of pestle or use a blender. Filter the homogenised mixture through the muslin cloth.
2. Now, pour the filtrate into a test tube.
3. Break the cell wall of the plant cell by treating the material with the enzyme cellulase.
4. Now, the same material is treated with enzyme protease to remove histone proteins (which are associated with DNA).
5. Then, add some amount of ribonuclease in it to dissolve the associated RNA followed by addition of lipase to dissolve the lipids present in the sample.
6. Gradually pour twice the volume of ice-cold 95% ethanol into the test tube. This causes the DNA to precipitate out of the solution.
7. The precipitated DNA can then be spooled with the help of a glass rod.

Isolated DNA

Spooling of DNA

**Fig. 5.1** Isolation of DNA from plant and spooling of DNA

## Observations

White thin DNA strands can be seen in the solution. This DNA represents the DNA found in the plant cells.

## Result

DNA appears as white precipitate of very fine threads on the spool.

### PRECAUTIONS

- *Fresh plant materials should be used for the extraction of DNA.*
- *The glasswares must be throughly cleaned and dried before the experiment.*
- *The enzymes and chemicals used for the experiment should be of standard quality.*
- *Chemicals and solutions should be used carefully in order to avoid any wastage.*

# Viva-Voce

**Q.1 Who gave the double helical structure of DNA?**

**Ans** Watson and Crick gave the double helical structure of DNA based on X-ray diffraction data.

**Q.2 What is the need of extracting DNA?**

**Ans** Extracted DNA can be analysed further for better understanding of the genetic make up of an organism.

**Q.3 What is the role of cellulase enzyme in extracting DNA?**

**Ans** The enzyme cellulase helps in the digestion of cellulosic cell wall of the plant cell.

**Q.4 Name three major steps involved in DNA extraction.**

**Ans** Three major steps involved in DNA extraction are:

(i) Homogenisation (ii) Deproteinisation (iii) Spooling.

**Q.5 What does the DNA look like on extraction?**

**Ans** DNA appears as white precipitate of very fine threads on the glass rod or spool.

**Q.6 What are the building blocks of nucleic acid?**

**Ans** The nucleotides are the building blocks of nucleic acid which consists of nitrogen containing aromatic base attached to a pentose sugar (five carbon) that is in turn attached to a phosphate group.

**Q.7 How is DNA different from RNA?**

**Ans**

| DNA | RNA |
|---|---|
| Found in the nucleus of most of the organisms. | Found mainly in the viruses. |
| Double-stranded structure. | Single-stranded structure. |
| Pentose sugar is deoxyribose. | Pentose sugar is ribose. |

**Q.8 Give the components of homogenisation media.**

**Ans** Homogenisation media consists of

(i) Sodium Dodecyl Sulphate (SDS) (ii) Ethylene Diamine Tetraacetic Acid (EDTA)

(iii) Sodium Chloride (NaCl) (non-iodised)

**Q.9 In which part of the cell is DNA present/found? Where can RNA be found in a cell?**

**Ans** DNA is found in the nucleus, mitochondria and in chloroplast (plant) of a cell. The nucleic acid, RNA is found in the cytoplasm and nucleoplasm of a cell depending on whether the cell is prokaryotic or eukaryotic.

**Q.10 Why the ice-chilled condition should be preferred for isolating DNA?**

**Ans** The ice-chilled conditions help to slow down the activity of enzyme that breakdown DNA and thereby help to increase the yield of DNA.

**Q.11 Name different nitrogenous bases present in the nucleic acid.**

**Ans** There are two types of nitrogenous bases present in the nucleic acid. These are:

(i) **Purines** Adenine and guanine.

(ii) **Pyrimidines** Cytosine, uracil and thymine. Uracil is present only in RNA while thymine is present in DNA in place of uracil.

**Q.12 What is the difference between nucleoside and nucleotide?**

**Ans** Nucleoside is made up of pentose sugar and nitrogenous base, while nucleotide is made up of pentose sugar, nitrogenous base and phosphate group.

SECTION-B

# Experiment 1

## AIM

To study adaptations of flowers pollinated by different agencies (wind, insects and birds).

## Theory/Principle

A typical flower is a modified shoot and serves as the reproductive organ of an angiosperm. It bears both male and female reproductive organs, producing male gametes (i.e. pollen grains) and female gamete (i.e. egg cell) respectively.

### Pollination

It is the process of transfer of pollen grains from anther of stamen to the receptive stigma of either same flower or another flower of the same species. The pollen grains are brought to the stigma by many different agencies such as wind, water, insects and birds. This phenomenon is considered as an important event in the sexually reproducing plants. In nature, it occurs by three methods:

**Autogamy or Self-pollination**

It is a type of pollination in which pollens gets transferred to the stigma of the same flower.

**Geitonogamy**

It is the type of pollination that occurs between the different flowers borne on the same plant.

**Xenogamy or Cross-pollination**

This type of pollination occurs when pollens are transferred from the flower of one plant to the flower of another plant of same species through various agents like wind, insect and water. Each flower shows special adaptative features to different pollinating agencies. Various method of cross-pollination are listed below

(i) **Anemophily** When pollination occurs with the help of wind, it is called anemophily. Examples-grasses, bamboo, coconut, palms, date palm, maize, *Pinus, Cannabis* and sugarcane.

(ii) **Entomophily** When pollination occurs with the help of insects, it is called entomophily. Example-*Salvia,* Rose, *Magnolia, Bougainvillea* and *Helianthus* (sunflower).

(iii) **Ornithophily** Pollination by birds is called ornithophily. Examples-*Agave, Bignonia, Bombax* and *Callistemon.*

(iv) **Hydrophily** When pollination occurs with the help of water, it is called hydrophily. Examples-*Vallisneria, Zostera* and *Hydrilla.*

## Requirements

Compound microscope, hand lens, forceps, needle, slides, coverslip, fresh flowers of maize or grass, *Salvia, Bignonia,* etc.

## Procedure

1. Firstly, select atleast one flower of each category (wind, insect, and bird) pollinated.
2. Observe its morphological characteristics and note down the adaptations of the flower in its structure which facilitate pollination by external agencies.
3. Dissect it out to observe its male and female reproductive parts.
4. Dust the pollens on a drop of water on slide and observe its characteristics under the microscope.
5. Finally draw a labelled diagram of adaptive features of flowers of each category.

## Observations

### Adaptations of the plants to wind pollination (Anemophily)

#### i. Maize *(Zea mays)*

1. Maize plant bears male and female flowers separately on the same plant. Male flowers are terminal whereas, female flowers are axillary in position.
2. Flowers are small, inconspicuous, colourless, odourless and nectarless.
3. Both stigma and anthers hang outside the perianth (exserted in position).
4. Pollens are light, small and dusty. They are produced in large numbers.
5. Stigma is large, feathery and sticky to in catch wind dispersed pollens.

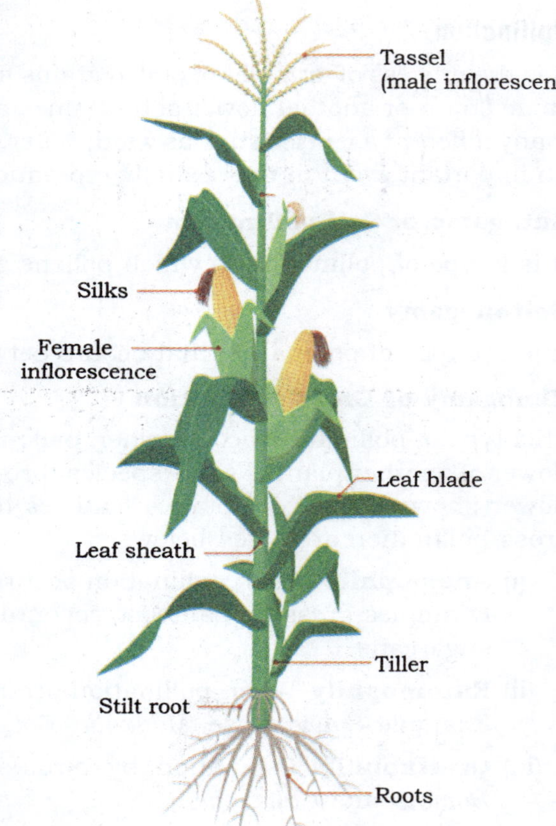


**Fig. 1.1** Maize has anemophilous flower

#### ii. *Pinus* (Pine)

1. The pollens are produced in huge numbers.
2. They are light weight.
3. The pollen possesses wings, which help them to move along the with wind to far-off places.

#### iii. Grasses (Wheat and Rice)

1. Flowers are not brightly coloured or showy and are inconspicuous in nature.
2. They lack scent and dot not secrete any nectar, but produce light weight pollen grains in large numbers.
3. Stigma is feathery to catch pollen.

## Adaptations of the plants to insect pollination (Entomophily)

### *Salvia*

1. The flowers are showy, brightly coloured and attract insects like honeybees.
2. They are borne on verticillaster inflorescence to become conspicuous.
3. Corolla is gamopetalous and two-lipped (bilabiate). The lower lip provides a landing platform for the insects.
4. Each flower has two epipetalous stamens in which a stamen is attached to the petal by filament.
5. Stamens have special modifications which help insects to pollinate flowers.
6. One of the anther lobe is sterile and the other is fertile. Both lobes are separated apart by a long connective tissue.
7. The upper arm of connective tissue bears fertile anther lobe and lower bears sterile anther lobe.
8. When an insect lands on lower lip of flower to collect nectar, the sterile anther lobe is pushed down, which brings fertile lobe down in contact with the body of the insect thus, dusting pollen on it.
9. When this pollen loaded insect visits another mature flower, the style brings stigma in such a position that it brushes against the back of the insect and collects pollen grains brought by the insect from a mature flower.

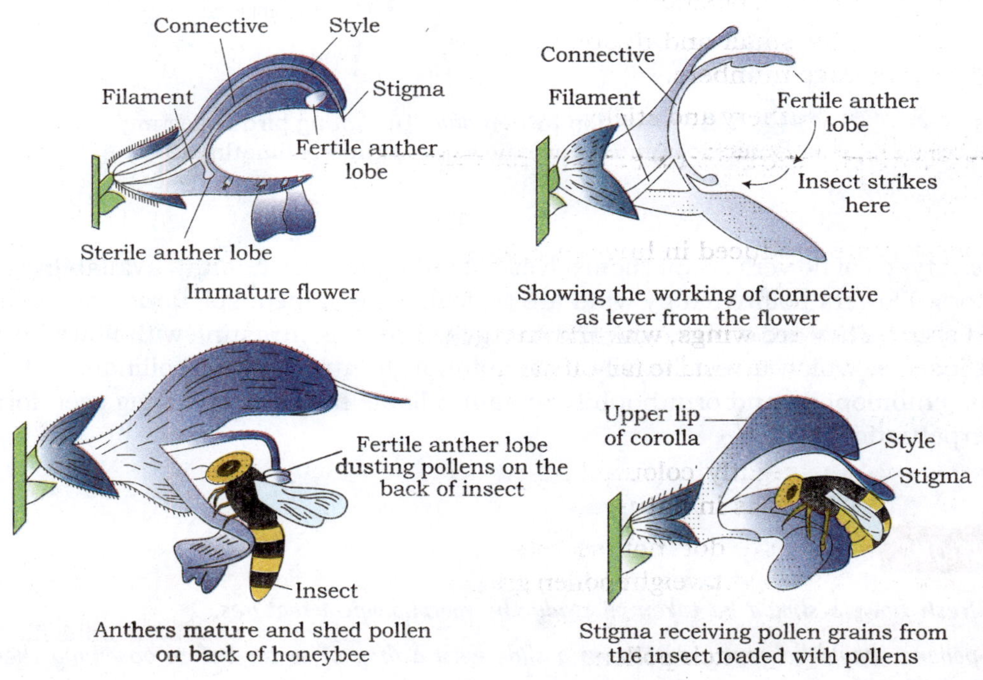


**Fig. 1.2** *Salvia* flower being pollinated by honeybee

## Adaptations of plants to bird pollination (Ornithophily)

### *Bignonia*

1. The flowers are big and brightly coloured-red, orange, yellow or blue.
2. The floral parts are thick and leathery especially corolla.
3. The flowers produce abundant nectar and may also have certain edible parts. Birds visit flowers for feeding on this nectar.
4. The flowers are usually odourless (without any fragrance or scent).

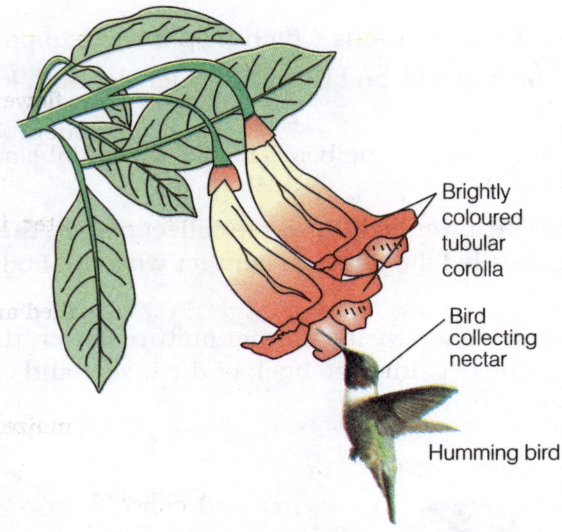


**Fig. 1.3** Pollination in *Bignonia* (Humming bird collecting nectar from *Bignonia* flower and thus pollinating it)

## Result

The different types of flowers adapt themselves according to their habitat, availability and the type of pollinators. Flowers pollinated by wind are typically small, inconspicuous, lack vibrant colour, nectar and scent. They are economical and energy efficient, contrasting with flowers pollinated by birds and insects, which invest heavily in adaptation to attract their pollinators. Despite these differences, entomophily and ornithophily remain reliable methods ensuring seed formation and species perpetuation.

### PRECAUTIONS

- *The fresh flowers should be taken to study the morphological features.*
- *The pollens should be gently dusted on a slide with a drop of water before observing them under the microscope.*

## Viva-Voce

**Q.1 Define autogamy.**

**Ans** It is the type of pollination in which pollen pollinate the stigma of the same flower borne on the same plant.

**Q.2 What is xenogamy?**

**Ans** It is a kind of pollination in which pollens of one plant/flower pollinate the flower of other plant of the same species. It requires the involvement of various external agencies such as wind, water, insects, etc.

**Q.3 How is autogamy different from xenogamy?**

**Ans** In autogamy, the pollen grain reaches to the stigma of same flower whereas, in xenogamy pollination occurs between the flowers of different plants, but of the same species.

**Q.4 Name the different agents of pollination.**

**Ans** The plants are pollinated by various agents such as wind, water, insects, birds and animals.

**Q.5 What are anemophilous flowers?**

**Ans** The flowers in which pollination occurs through wind are called anemophilous flowers and this phenomenon is called anemophily.

**Q.6 Give examples of anemophilous flowers.**

**Ans** All grasses, *Cannabis*, sugarcane, bamboo, coconut, *Pinus*, maize, etc. have anemophilous flowers.

**Q.7 How does pollination occur in wheat and rice?**

**Ans** Wheat and rice get pollinated by wind.

**Q.8 How does pollination occur in *Salvia*?**

**Ans** The pollination is done mostly by honeybees in *Salvia*.

**Q.9 What is ornithophily?**

**Ans** The pollination done by birds is called ornithophily, e.g. *Callistemon* (bottle brush plant), ***Bombax malabarica***, *Agave* and *Bignonia*.

**Q.10 Why is cross-pollination preferred over self-pollination?**

**Ans** The cross pollination brings about the variability in the successive generation by the phenomenon of heterosis.

**Q.11 How do flowers that bloom at night get pollinated?**

**Ans** Flowers that bloom at night get pollinated by nocturnal insects like moths and beetles and sometimes by bats.

**Q.12 Why do anemophilous flowers produce pollen in huge numbers?**

**Ans** The wind pollinated flowers produce large number of pollens because chances of pollen being wasted are higher.

**Q.13 Why does wheat have feathery stigma?**

**Ans** The feathery stigma helps to catch wind borne pollens of wheat to bring about pollination in the plant.

**Q.14 The flowers of some plants are brightly coloured and also produce scent. What is the likelihood of pollination agency in this flower?**

**Ans** The brightly coloured flowers having scent generally attract insects. In this process, they bring about pollination. So, these flowers are pollinated by insects.

# Experiment 2

## AIM

To study the pollen germination on stigma through a permanent slide or scanning electron micrograph.

## Theory/Principle

The pollen grains are the male gametophytes in angiosperms. These are produced in anthers as a result of a process called **microsporogenesis**. The microspore mother cell in anthers divides meiotically to produce tetrad of pollens, each having haploid number of chromosomes. A pollen grain is surrounded by two wall layers, i.e. an outer exine and inner intine.

### Exine

It is the outer tough protective layer made up of **sporopollenin**, which is the most resistant biological material known so far. At some places exine is either very thin or absent. Such regions in exine are called **germ pores**.

### Intine

It is the inner smooth layer made up of pectocellulose deposition in its wall. Intine gives rise to pollen tube through germ pores present in exine. Before the discharge from microsporangium, each pollen grain possess a large vegetative cell and a small generative cell as shown in figure below:

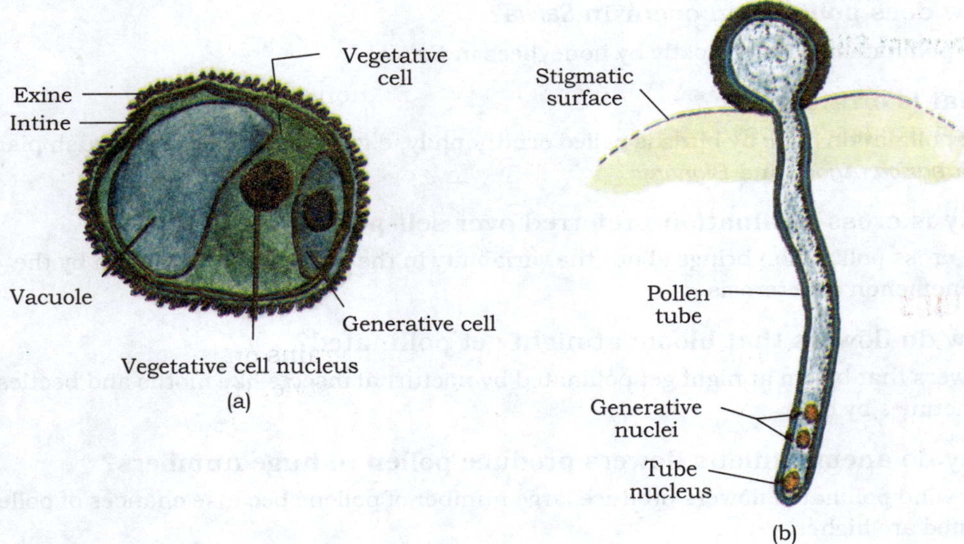


**Fig. 2.1** (a) Structure of pollen grain, (b) Pollen germination on stigma

The generative cell later divides to form two male gametes. The pollen germination is initiated by certain chemicals present on the stigma and the growth of the pollen tube (made up of cellulose) is supported by sugary substances secreted by the cells of stigma. The pollen tube emerges out through one of the germ pore and passes through the tissues of stigma and style to reach the ovule and discharge its male gametes. One male gamete fuses with the egg cell and the other male gamete fuses with polar nuclei of the female gametophyte. This phenomenon is called **double fertilisation**, a characteristic feature of all angiosperms.

## Requirements

Permanent slide or scanning electron micrographs of pollen germination with stigma, compound microscope, drawing sheets, pencil and an eraser. For temporary slide preparation 5-6 excised styles with stigma of *Petunia*/grass/maize/sunflower, beaker, water, slides, coverslips, dropper, cotton blue stain, glycerine, brush and needle.

## Procedure

### Using Temporary Slide

1. Place the freshly excised stigma and styles in boiling water in a beaker for about 5-10 minutes. This will soften the tissues and also prevent them from drying.
2. Add cotton blue dye using a dropper onto the tissue placed on a glass slide.
3. Wait for 3-5 minutes and then wash-off the excess stain with water.
4. Mount one stigma in a drop of glycerine on a slide.
5. Place a coverslip on stigma and gently press the coverslip on the material.
6. Place the temporary slide under a compound microscope and observe it initially under low magnification followed by higher magnification. If you fail to observe pollen tubes, mount another stigma.
7. Draw a well-labelled diagram of the structures seen.

### Using Permanent Slide

1. Pick up a good permanent slide of pollen germination.
2. Place it under low power microscope and observe the slide.
3. Then switch to high power to have clear view of the details of pollen tube or observe the scanning electron micrographs of pollen germination on stigma.
4. Draw a well-labelled diagram of the structures seen.

## Observations

The slide shows the presence of many germinating pollen grains on the stigma of the carpel. The pollen tubes of the germinating pollen grows through the style, transversing the tissues of the style. The slide shows many such growing pollen tubes of varied length.

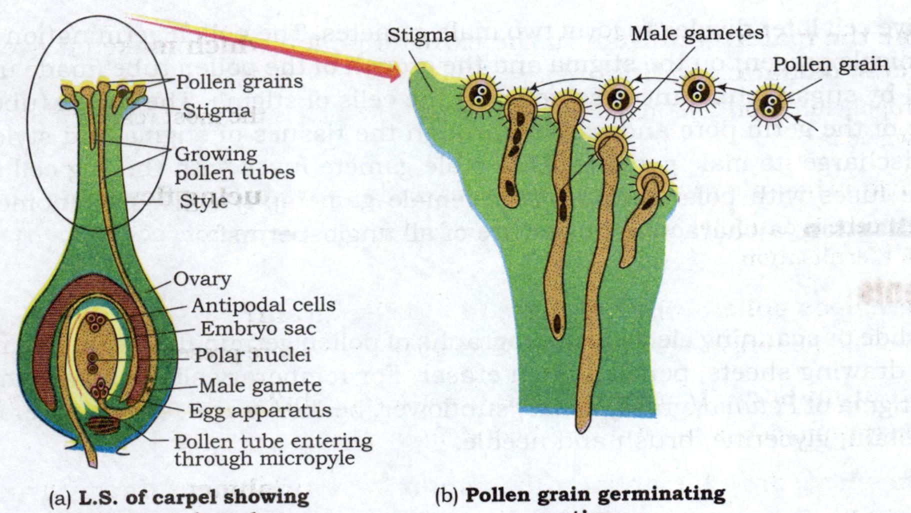


(a) **L.S. of carpel showing stigma, style and ovary**

(b) **Pollen grain germinating on stigma**

**Fig. 2.2** Germination of pollen grain

## Result/Conclusion

As the pollen tube grows into style, it reaches ovule and carries the two male gametes; one to the egg cell and another to secondary nucleus for fertilisation that occur inside the ovule.

### PRECAUTIONS

- *The permanent slide should be carefully handled.*
- *Proper figures of the structures as seen under low and higher magnifications of the compound microscope should be drawn.*
- *Figures should be accurately labelled.*

## Viva-Voce

**Q.1 What are pollen grains?**

**Ans** Pollen grains are the microspores that represents the male gametophyte.

**Q.2 Name the cells present in the pollen grain.**

**Ans** A pollen grain possesses a tube cell (vegetative cell) and a generative cell.

**Q.3 Which part of pollen forms the pollen tube?**

**Ans** The intine wall of pollen grain gives rise to pollen tube after germination.

**Q.4 What are germpores?**

**Ans** Germpores are the places where exine is either very thin or absent.

**Q.5 Do all pollen tubes reach the ovules?** NCERT

**Ans** No, all pollen tubes does not reaches to the ovule.

**Q.6 Name the material present in the exine of pollen which makes it overcome adverse climatic conditions.**

**Ans** Sporopollenin is present in the exine of the pollen which is the most resistant biological material known so far.

**Q.7 Mention the role of pollen tube in sexually reproducing flowering plants.**

**Ans** Pollen tube is a tubular structure that transport male gametes from pollen grains to the embryo sac for fertilisation.

**Q.8 Where does pollen tube originate in a pollen grain?**

**Ans** The pollen tube originates from intine through the germ pore present in the exine.

**Q.9 What stimulates the germination of pollen grain?**

**Ans** Pollen germination is stimulated by hydration on stigma.

**Q.10 From where does the pollen tube obtain its nourishment during growth?**

**Ans** Pollen tube obtains its nourishment from the transmitting tissue of the style during its growth.

**Q.11 Are all pollen tubes of equal length? If not, why.** NCERT

**Ans** No, pollen tubes are not of equal length because the newly germinated pollen will have shorter tube as compared to older germinated pollen which have comparatively longer pollen tube.

**Q.12 Name the part of gynoecium that determines the compatible nature of pollen.**

**Ans** Stigmatic tissue determines the compatibility of a pollen.

**Q.13 Can pollen grains of one plant species germinate on stigma of other species? Give reason.** NCERT

**Ans** Pollen grain of one plant species will not germinate on the stigma of other species because of pollen incompatibility.

**Q.14 Are all pollen grains capable of fertilisation?**

**Ans** No, not all pollen grains are capable of undergoing fertilisation as some may be non-viable or genetically incompatible, which prevents successful fertilisation.

**Q.15 What is the most reliable method for assessing the viability of pollen grains?**

**Ans** Pollen germination is the most reliable method for assessing the viability of pollen grains.

# Experiment 3

## AIM

To identify the stages of gamete development, i.e. T.S. of testis and T.S. of ovary through permanent slides (from grasshopper/mice).

## Theory/Principle

Gametes are the haploid ($n$) cells involved in the process of sexual reproduction.

The process of formation of male and female gametes, i.e. sperms in males and ova in females is called **gametogenesis**.

The process of gametogenesis includes certain phases of development and maturation of gametes. This process takes place in different organs in males and females. In males, it occurs in the testes and in female, it occurs in the ovaries. Both of these organs are known as primary sex organs.

### Testis

In mammals, a pair of testes are present in scrotum lying outside the abdomen. Sperms formation occurs inside the testis by the process of **spermatogenesis**.

The events involved in spermatogenesis are summarised below

**Multiplication phase**

Cells of germinal epithelium ($2n$) of seminiferous tubule divide by mitosis.

↓ Mitosis differentiation

**Maturation phase**

Primary spermatocytes ($2n$) undergo first stage of reductional division.

↓ Meiosis-I

Secondary spermatocytes ($n$) undergo second stage of reductional division.

↓ Meiosis-II

Spermatids ($n$) are formed. These are spherical and non-dividing cells.

↓ Differentiation

**Spermiogenesis**

Spermatozoa ($n$) formed are elongated and non-dividing cells which are eventually called the male gametes.

### Ovary

Mammalian ovaries are paired, almond-shaped and solid structures found in the female body. Formation of ova, i.e. oogenesis takes place inside them. The events involved in oogenesis are summarised below:

**Multiplication phase**
Cells of germinal epithelium ($2n$) of ovary undergo mitotic division.
↓ Mitosis
Oogonia ($2n$) are formed within the fetal ovary.
↓ Initiation of meiosis I

**Growth phase**
Primary oocytes ($2n$) are formed and get surrounded by granulosa cells. They are temporarily arrested at meiosis-I
↓ Completion of Meiosis-I

**Maturation phase**
A large secondary oocyte ($n$) and a small polar body ($n$) is formed.
↓ Meiosis-II
Single ovum ($n$) and second polar body is formed ($n$).

## Requirements

Permanent slides of T.S. of testis and ovary of mouse, compound microscope, notebook, pencil, eraser, lens cleaning fluid and cleaning paper.

## Procedure

1. First, clean the slide and microscope lens with the help of lens cleaning paper and cleaning fluid.
2. Fix the slide on the stage of microscope.
3. Observe the slide of testis and ovary of mouse first under the low power magnification and then under higher magnification.
4. Now, draw the labelled diagrams as seen in the sections of both testis and ovary.

## Observation

### T.S. of Mammalian Testis

#### Identification Characteristics

1. The seminiferous tubules are easily seen in the cross-section of testis embedded in interstitial tissues. These appear as coiled, circular structures.
2. The presence of larger cells called sertoli cell is the characteristic feature of this slide.
3. The presence of interstitial cells or Leydig's cell is evident.

#### General Characteristics

1. Each seminiferous tubule is lined on its inside by germinal epithelium which divides mitotically to produce male germ cells called **spermatogonia**.
2. Various stages of development of sperm, from spermatogonia to spermatozoa, are seen from periphery to the lumen of seminiferous tubules. The sequence of stages of its development is as follows:

$$\underset{(2n)}{\text{Spermatogonia}} \xrightarrow{\text{Mitosis}} \underset{(2n)}{\text{Primary spermatocyte}} \xrightarrow{\text{Meiosis-I}}$$

$$\underset{(n)}{\text{Secondary spermatocyte}} \xrightarrow{\text{Meiosis-II}} \underset{(n)}{\text{Spermatids}} \rightarrow \underset{(n)}{\text{Spermatozoa}}$$

3. All these stages are clearly visible in a transverse section of testis. The mature sperms are present in the centre, primary spermatocyte in the middle layer and spermatogonia towards the periphery of seminiferous tubules.
4. **Sertoli cells** are prominent pyramid-shaped cells found in between the germinal cells. These cells provide nutrition to the developing spermatozoa.
5. **Leydig cells** are seen in the interstitial tissue. They produce the hormone called **testosterone** responsible for development of male secondary sexual characters.

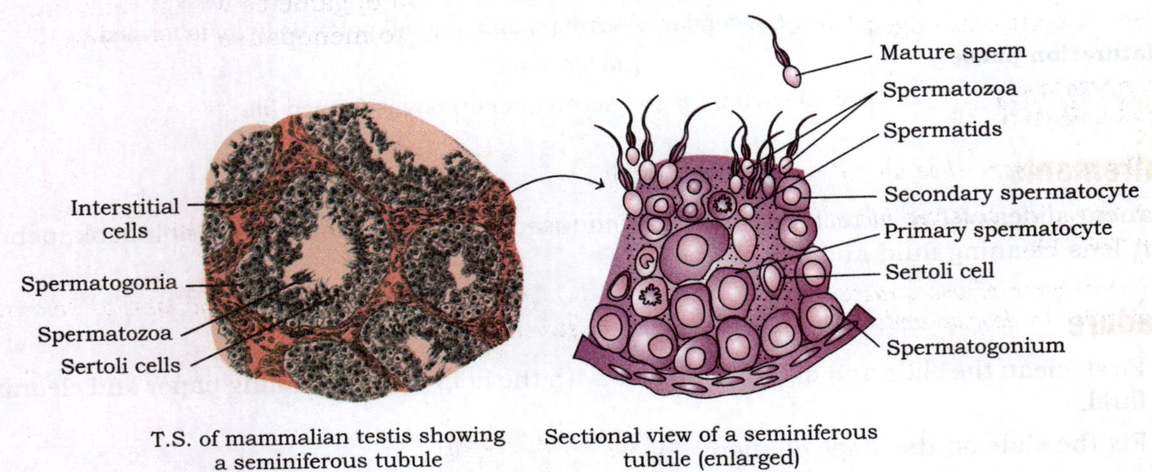


**Fig. 3.1** TS of mammalian testis

## T.S. of Mammalian Ovary

### Identification Characteristics

1. The presence of Graafian follicle is a characteristic feature of a mammalian ovary.
2. Each Graafian follicle contains one ovum, a cavity called antrum as well as granulosa and theca cells.

### General Characteristics

1. The section of mammalian ovary shows the mass of tissues lined up by germinal epithelium.
2. The stroma is made up of connective tissue, blood vessels and nerve fibres.
3. Various circular structures seen in stroma are **Graafian follicles**, in their various developmental stages like primary and secondary oocytes.
4. In the later stages of follicular development, a fluid-filled cavity called **antrum** appears which separates the ovum and the cells around it except at one point.

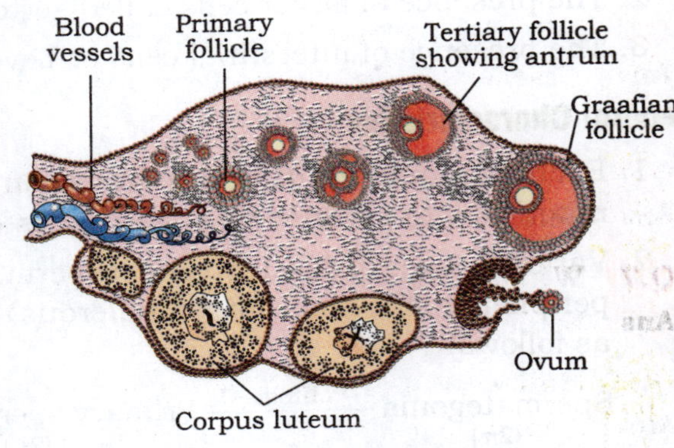


**Fig. 3.2** TS of ovary

5. As this cavity enlarges, Graafian follicle (mature follicle) becomes ready to release ovum.

6. The mature follicle ruptures and releases ovum (ovulation). The ruptured follicles form **corpus luteum** (which is an endocrine tissue) and release **progesterone** (the pregnancy hormone).

## Result/Conclusion

The transverse sections of testis and ovary of mice (mammal) clearly show the developmental stages of sperms and ova by the process of gametogenesis. Spermatogenesis is a continuous process that begins at puberty, leading to ongoing development of gametes within seminiferous tubules. In contrast, oogenesis spans from fetal development to menopause in ovaries.

### PRECAUTIONS

- *The permanent slide should be handled carefully.*
- *It should be observed initially under the low and then under the higher magnification of the microscope.*
- *The diagram of the structures seen in T.S. of ovary and testis should be drawn and labelled properly in order to develop understanding of the detailed structures.*

## Viva-Voce

**Q.1 What is gametogenesis?**
**Ans** It is a process by which male and female gametes, i.e. sperms and ova are formed in the testis and ovary of mammals, respectively.

**Q.2 What is spermatozoa?**
**Ans** The mammalian male gamete is called spermatozoa.

**Q.3 What is the function of Sertoli cells?**
**Ans** Sertoli cells provide nutrition to the developing spermatozoa.

**Q.4 What is the function of Leydig cells?**
**Ans** Leydig cells produces male sex hormone named testosterone.

**Q.5 What is corpus luteum?**
**Ans** Graafian follicle releases its ovum at maturity and empty Graafian follicle becomes endocrine gland called corpus luteum.

**Q.6 What is the role of seminiferous tubule?**
**Ans** Seminiferous tubule are the site of production of sperms in testes.

**Q.7 What products are produced by the ruptured Graafian follicle?**
**Ans** Secondary oocyte and corpus luteum are produced by the ruptured Graafian follicle.

**Q.8 How can sperm cell be identified under a microscope in the slide?**
**Ans** A sperm is present in the lumen of seminiferous tubule and has a tail at one end.

**Q.9** **Draw a labelled diagram of TS of testis.** NCERT

**Ans** Refer to page no. 46.

**Q.10** **Draw a labelled diagram of TS of ovary.** NCERT

**Ans** Refer to page no. 46.

**Q.11** **What are different parts of spermatozoa?**

**Ans** Spermatozoa bears a head, neck, middle piece and a tail.

**Q.12** **What would happen if meiosis fails to occur in gametocyte?** NCERT

**Ans** If meiosis fails to occur in gametocyte then the gamete will have two sets of chromosomes and this will result in the chromosomal aberration.

**Q.13** **At which stage of follicular development, is ovum released?** NCERT

**Ans** The mature Graafian follicle ruptures and releases ovum in the middle of the menstrual cycle, i.e. 14-16th day. This is called ovulatory phase.

**Q.14** **Spermatogenesis is a continuous process. Justify the statement.** NCERT

**Ans** Spermatogenesis is a continuous process because it occurs throughout a male's reproductive life, from puberty till old age.

**Q.15** **What would happen if sperms are devoid of their tails?** NCERT

**Ans** The tail of sperm is important for its movement to reach the ovum. Any default in the structure of sperm will make it worthless and unable to reach to the ovum.

**Q.16** **What are the consequences of failure of ovulation?** NCERT

**Ans** The process of ovulation makes ovum available for fertilisation. If ovulation does not occur, there will be no fertilisation and there will be no pregnancy or reproduction.

**Q.17** **When does follicular development begins in a girl child?**

**Ans** Follicular development in a girl begins during the foetal development.

# Experiment 4

## AIM

To study meiosis in onion bud cell or grasshopper testis using permanent slides.

## Theory/Principle

### Meiosis

Meiosis is a type of cell division that occurs in the reproductive cells of sexually reproducing organisms. This division is responsible for producing gametes in animals (sperm and ovum) and in plants (pollen and egg). In this type of cell division, the number of chromosomes in daughter cells is reduced to half, hence it is also called the **reductional division**.

It comprises of mainly two phases, i.e. **meiosis-I** and **meiosis-II**.

### Meiosis-I

It is the reductional division in which the chromosomes of homologous pairs separate from each other. Two important events occur in meiosis-I, which are as follows:

(i) **Synaptonemal complex formation** occurs between the homologous chromosome during prophase-I of meiosis.

(ii) **Crossing over** is considered as the important event of meiosis-I as it brings about variation in the offsprings produced thus helping in evolution. Process of crossing over facilitates the exchange of genetic material between non-sister chromatids of homologous chromosomes. As a result of this, new recombinant chromosomes are formed which differ from the parental ones and are inherited by the next generation through gametes.

### Meiosis-II

It is an equational division that results in the formation of four daughter cells. In this division, chromosome number remains same as produced in meiosis-I. It is initiated immediately after **cytokinesis** of meiosis-I.

Meiosis can be observed in a cytological preparation of the cells of testis tubules or in the pollen mother cells of the anthers of flower buds.

## Requirements

Permanent slides of all the stages of meiotic division in onion bud or testis of grasshopper and compound microscope.

## Procedure

1. Place the clean permanent slide on the stage of compound microscope.
2. Focus the slide under low power (10x) of the microscope and search for the dividing cell.
3. When divided cells are located observe them under higher magnification.
4. Use pointer in the objective lens to point out a specific stage of meiotic cell division.
5. Observe the stage of the cell pointed by pointer under high power (45x) of the microscope.
6. Draw the figure as seen in the microscope and write comments in the practical file.

## Observations

A significant number of cells were in the interphase. These cells have a centrally positioned densely stained nucleus. Apart from that, different stages of meiosis were also observed under the microscope. These cells have different special features which are summarised below:

## Meiosis-I (First Nuclear Division)

### i. Prophase-I

It is a complex phase characterised by number of events. It is divided into five main sub-stages:

(a) **Leptotene** (*leptos* – slender; *tene* – band or thread)

1. Nuclear membrane and nucleolus are still distinctly observable.
2. Fine network of thin chromatin are seen in the nucleus. These fibres may be observed in the condensed form during the later stages and are then called chromosomes.

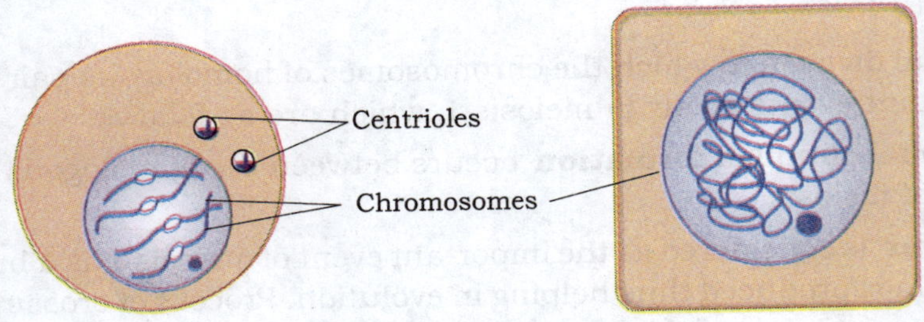


**Fig. 4.1** Leptotene

(b) **Zygotene** (*zygon* – paired)

1. Pairing of homologous chromosomes occurs in this stage and this process is called synapsis. The complex formed by a pair of synapsed homologous chromosome is called a bivalent.

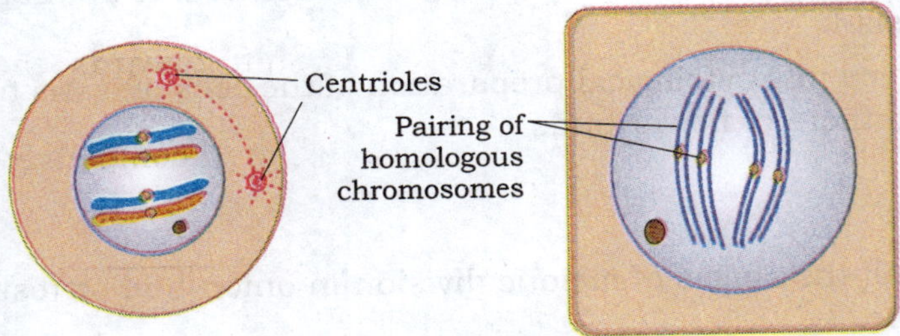


**Fig. 4.2** Zygotene

2. Chromosomes becomes more distinct as they become much shorter than before.

(c) **Pachytene** (*pachy* – thick)

1. The chromatin threads get condensed and appear shortened and thick.
2. The homologous pairs of chromosomes are clearly visible.
3. Each chromosome has two chromatids, so each bivalent consists of four chromatids. Hence, the chromosomes exhibit **tetrad configuration**.

4. Crossing over, i.e. exchange of chromatid segments between non-sister chromatids of homologous chromosomes takes place at this stage.

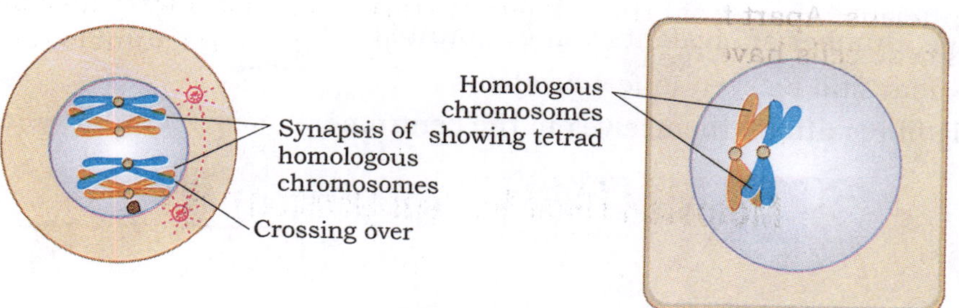


**Fig. 4.3** Pachytene

(d) **Diplotene** (*diplos* – double)

1. Each homologous chromosome has two chromatids that shows distinct separation from each other except at some points where attachments are seen.
2. These attachment points of two homologous chromosomes are called **chiasmata** (sing. chiasma).
3. These chiasmata represent the site of crossing over.

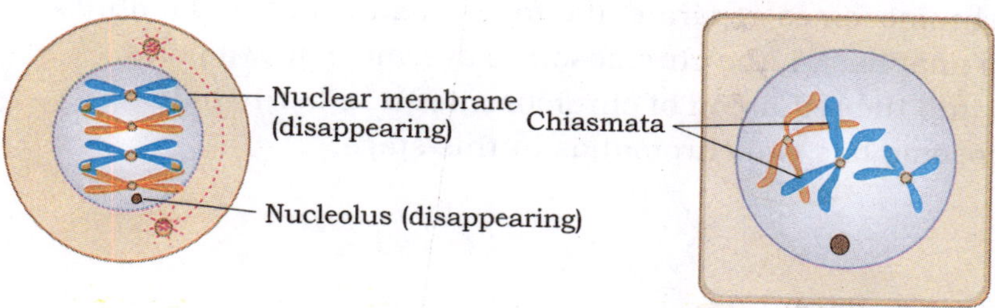


**Fig. 4.4** Diplotene

(e) **Diakinesis** (*dia* – opposite; *kinesis* – separation or movement)

1. Bivalents condense further during this stage and appear to be more shortened, thick and prominent than before.
2. Chiasmata are clearly visible. However, it shift towards the end of the paired chromosome, a process called terminalisation.
3. Nuclear membrane and nucleolus have disappeared completely.
4. Spindle formation can be seen in its early stages.

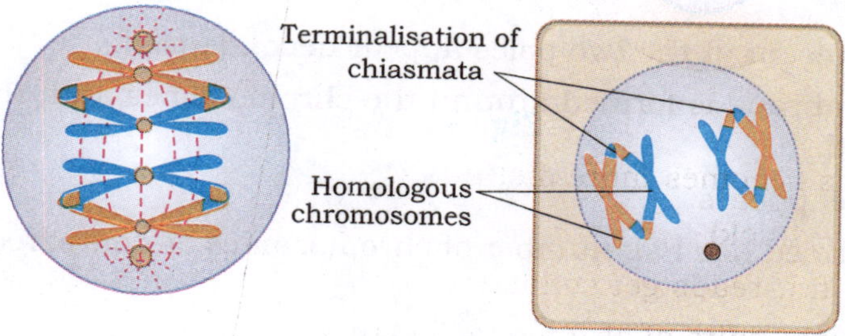


**Fig. 4.5** Diakinesis

### ii Metaphase-I

1. The homologous chromosomes are still in pairs and are arranged along the equatorial plane of the cell.
2. At this stage, number of bivalents can be counted.
3. Chiasmata may still be seen in few bivalents.
4. The spindle fibres attach themselves to the centromere of each chromosome pair.

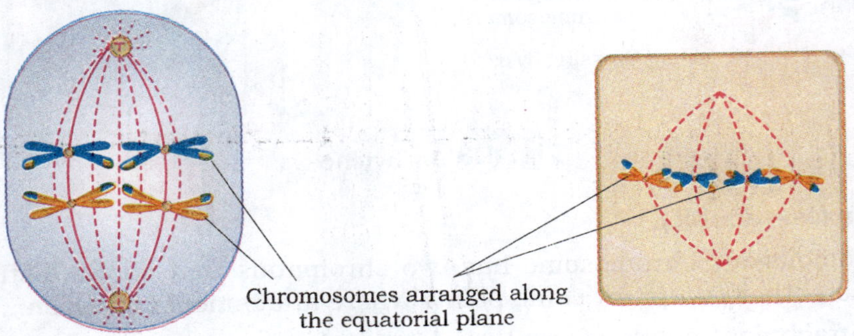


**Fig. 4.6** Metaphase-I

### iii Anaphase-I

1. The paired chromosomes separate due to shortening of spindle fibres.
2. At the end of anaphase-I, the chromosomes assemble at two poles.
3. This results into the reduction of chromosomes number to half.
4. Each chromosome has two chromatids at this stage.

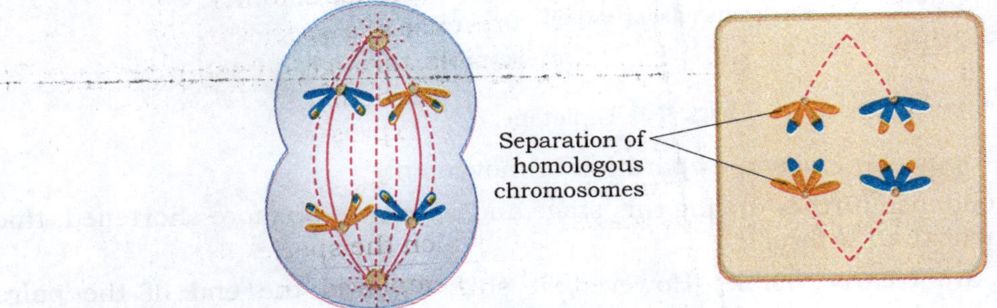


**Fig. 4.7** Anaphase-I

### iv Telophase-I

1. Chromosomes present at the two poles appear decondensed.
2. The nuclear membrane is formed around the chromosomes and, thus two new daughter nuclei are formed.
3. Nucleolus also reappears.
4. Each nucleus formed has half number of chromosomes as compared to the nucleus of the parent cell.

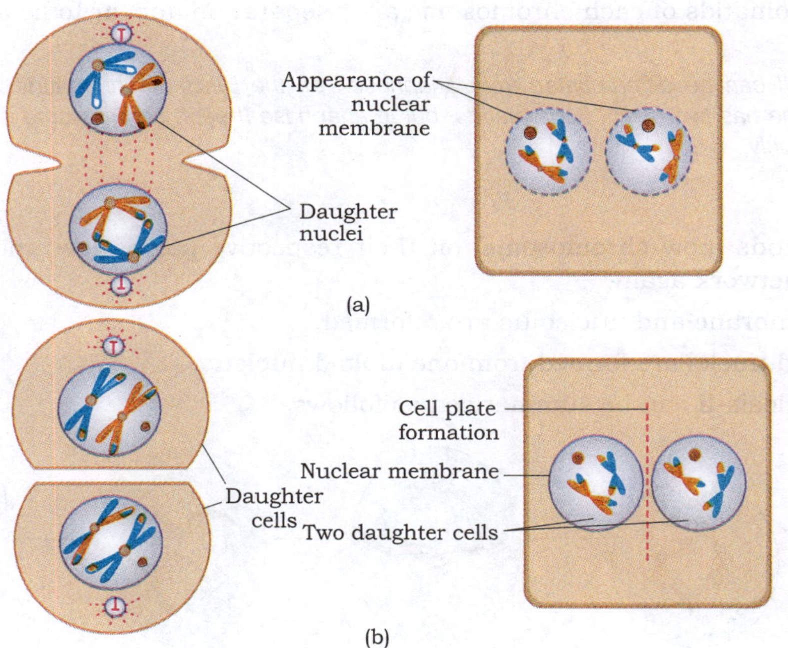


**Fig. 4.8** (a) Telophase-I (b) Cytokinesis

**Note** *It is not necessary that cytokinesis takes place after telophase-I. Cells can there after enter into the second meiotic division after meiosis-I.*

## Meiosis-II (Second Nuclear Division)

Meiosis-II is similar to mitosis without duplication of DNA. It is divided into following stages:

### i. Prophase-II

1. The chromosomes appear as distinct rod-shaped or thread-like chromatin fibres.
2. Each chromosome has two chromatids.
3. Nuclear membrane and nucleolus start disappearing.

### ii. Metaphase-II

1. This phase is similar to that of mitotic division.
2. The chromosomes having two chromatids attached at the centromere are observed arranged at the equatorial plane of the cell.

**Note** *Metaphase-II can be differentiated from metaphase-I by the following features:*

1. *Each chromosome of metaphase-II has two sister chromatids joined at the centromere, while in metaphase-I, each pair of homologous chromosomes have two chromatids, forming a tetrad.*
2. *In metaphase-I a few chiasmata are observed, while no chiasmata are observed during metaphase-II.*

### iii. Anaphase-II

1. The centromere of each chromosome divides into two, so that each chromatid gets its centromere.
2. Shortening of the spindle fibres occurs so that chromatids are pulled apart towards their respective poles.

3. The two chromatids of each chromosome after separation appear to lie at the two poles of the cell.

**Note** *Anaphase-II can be differentiated from anaphase-I on the basis of chromatids. In anaphase-I, each chromosome has two distinct chromatids, but in anaphase-II each chromosome is represented by one chromatid only.*

### iv. Telophase-II

1. The chromatids (now chromosome) on their respective poles, now uncoil and form the chromatin network again.
2. Nuclear membrane and nucleolus are reformed.
3. Four haploid nuclei are formed from one diploid nucleus.

The process of meiosis-II can be summarised as follows

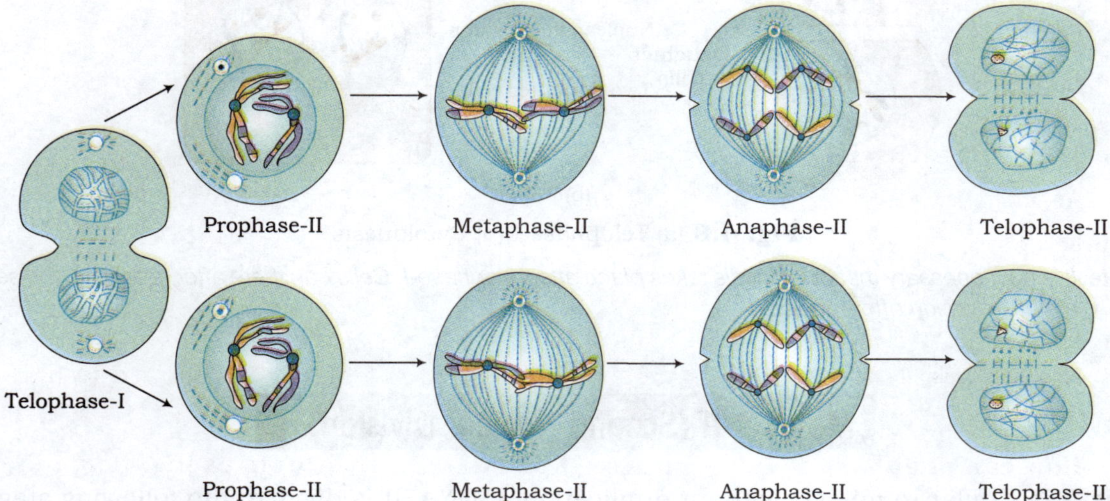


**Fig. 4.9** Stages of meiosis-II

## Result

The slides under observation revealed all the characteristic features of the meiotic cell division occurring in the onion bud or grasshopper testis.

### PRECAUTIONS

- *Handle the permanent slides cautiously so that they do not break.*
- *Focus each slide first under 10x magnification of light microscope and then under 45x magnification to get the better view of dividing cells.*

## Viva-Voce

**Q.1 What are germinal cells?**

**Ans** The cells present in the reproductive organs which take part in gamete formation are called germinal cells.

**Q.2 What is meiosis?**

**Ans** It is a kind of cell division, which occurs in diploid germinal cells to produce four haploid cells, each having half number of chromosomes as compared to parent cell.

**Q.3 How many daughter cells are produced at the end of meiosis?** NCERT

**Ans** Four haploid daughter cells are produced at the end of meiosis.

**Q.4 List two important events of meiosis.**

**Ans** (i) Crossing over

(ii) Formation of synaptonemal complex.

**Q.5 At what stages of meiosis, the chromosomes are best seen?**

**Ans** Metaphase-I and Metaphase-II.

**Q.6 Name the stages of meiosis where the nuclear membrane is not visible.**

**Ans** Metaphase-I, metaphase-II, anaphase-I and anaphase-II.

**Q.7 Name the stage of meiosis where the chromosome number is reduced to half.**

**Ans** Anaphase-I.

**Q.8 How can anaphase-I and anaphase-II be distinguished from each other?** NCERT

**Ans** The chromatid structure is the basis to differentiate anaphase-I from anaphase-II. In anaphase-I, each chromosome has two distinct chromatids, but in anaphase-II, each chromosome is represented by one chromatid only.

**Q.9 How can we identify a metaphase-I stage of meiosis in a slide?**

**Ans** The homologous chromosomes are arranged on the equatorial plate of a cell during metaphase-I.

**Q.10 At what stage of cell division does nuclear membrane reappear?**

**Ans** Telophase.

**Q.11 What is synapsis and crossing over?** NCERT

**Ans** Synapsis refers to the association of homologous chromosomes during zygotene stage of meiosis-I. Crossing over is the process of exchange of chromatid segments between non-sister chromatids of homologous chromosomes during pachytene of meiosis-I.

**Q.12 What is the purpose of using onion bud cell to study meiosis?**

**Ans** Onion bud cells are used to study meiosis because reproductive cell, which undergo meiosis, are present in abundance inside onion buds.

**Q.13 Which phase of meiosis has the longest duration?**

**Ans** Prophase I of meiosis I has the longest duration compared to other phases in meiosis.

**Q.14** **An organism has 22 pairs of chromosomes in its somatic cells. What will be the number of chromosomes in its gametes?**

**Ans** The gametes will have 11 chromosomes, i.e. haploid number (*n*).

**Q.15** **What is the significance of meiosis?** NCERT

**Ans** It is responsible for recombination of paternal and maternal genes in the gametes and it also maintains the constant number of chromosome in a species.

**Q.16** **Indicate distinguishing feature of metaphase-I of meiosis and metaphase of mitosis.** NCERT

**Ans** (i) Each chromosome of metaphase of mitosis has two chromatids whereas in metaphase-I of meiosis, these are paired homologous chromosomes each having two chromatids, thus forming a tetrad.

(ii) Metaphase of mitosis does not show any chiasmata whereas in metaphase-I of meiosis-I these can be seen.

**Q.17** **What is the significance of synapsis?** NCERT

**Ans** Synapsis is responible for creating sites for crossing over between two homologous chromosomes.

**Q.18** **The daughter cells produced at the end of meiosis are genetically different. Explain.** NCERT

**Ans** The crossing over phenomenon brings about genetic exchange between the homologous chromosomes. This results in genetic variations in the four daughter cells produced at the end of meiosis.

# Experiment 5

## AIM

To study the T.S. of blastula through permanent slide (mammalian).

## Theory/Principle

Sexually reproducing organisms produces male and female haploid gametes ($n$) which fertilises to form **zygote** ($2n$). Formation of zygote marks the beginning of a new life. The zygote undergoes mitotic divisions with no significant growth, by a process known as cleavage, leading to the development of blastomere. The zygote with 8-16 blastomeres is called morula.

This whole process occurs inside the Fallopian tube of female reproductive system. On the third day of fertilisation, the morula starts moving down the Fallopian tube to reach the uterus. The cells inside morula moves towards the periphery resulting in formation of a cavity (blastocoel). As soon as this cavity develops inside morula, it transforms into the blastocyst or blastula.

The cells in the blastula now differentiates into an outermost layer of cells called trophoblast and the inner cell mass. As blastula reaches the uterus, cells of trophoblast attaches with the wall of endometrium and the inner cell mass differentiates into the embryo. After attachment, the uterine cell divides rapidly and covers the blastocyst. As a result, the blastocyst becomes embedded in the endometrium of the uterus. This is called implantation. It happens on 6-9th day after fertilisation. The cells of inner mass get differentiated to form three germ layers, i.e. ectoderm, mesoderm and endoderm, this stage of embryo is called gastrula.

## Requirements

Permanent slide of T.S. of blastula, compound microscope, paper, pencil and eraser.

## Procedure

1. Select a good permanent slide of T.S. of blastula and focus it under 10x magnification using a compound microscope.
2. Now, study the structures and draw the different layers of cells as seen.
3. Finally compare these structures with the labelled diagrams given in the theory and identify them accordingly.

## Observations

The transverse section of blastula shows the following features

1. It appears as a spherical mass of cells.
2. A fluid filled cavity, called blastocoel is commonly seen inside the blastocyst.
3. The outermost layer of blastomeres called trophoblast is clearly seen.
4. Mass of cells inner to the trophoblast is called **inner cell mass**, responsible for the formation of embryo.

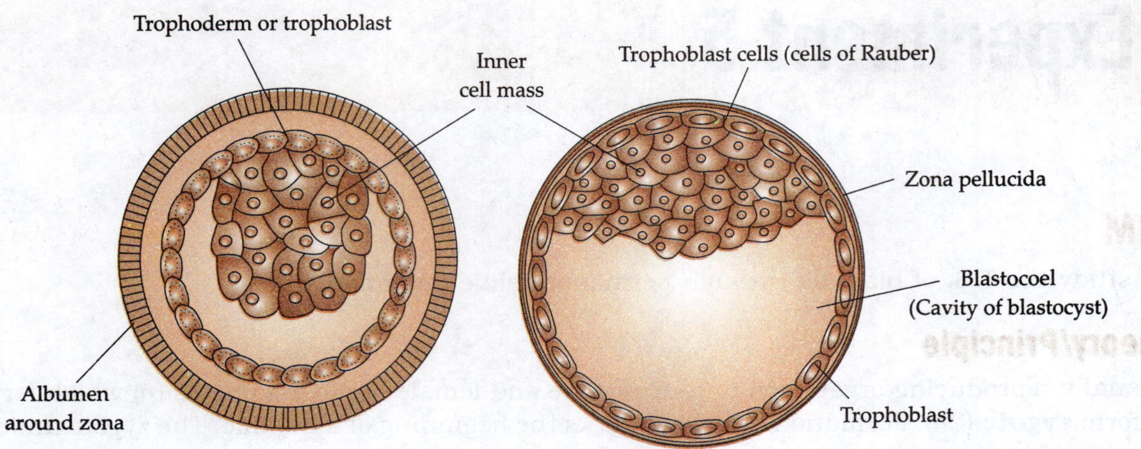


**Fig. 5.1** TS of blastula of a mammalian embryo

## Result

The transverse section of blastula clearly shows all characteristic features of blastula stage of a mammal.

### PRECAUTIONS

- *Objective and eye lenses should be cleaned before viewing the slide.*
- *The slide should be centrally placed so that it can be focused properly under the low and high powers of compound microscope in order to enhance the clear visibility of all cells.*

**Q.1 How does a zygote convert into morula?**

**Ans** The repeated mitotic cell divisions occurring in zygote changes it from a single cell to a multicellular (16-32 celled) structure called morula.

**Q.2 Where is morula formed in human female?**

**Ans** The formation of morula occurs in the Fallopian tube in human female.

**Q.3 What changes occur in morula to form blastocyst?**

**Ans** A cavity called blastocoel appears in morula because of movement of cells. At this stage, the blastocyst moves downward to come closer to the wall of uterus.

**Q.4 What are the differences between blastula and morula?** NCERT

**Ans**

| Morula | Blastula |
|---|---|
| It is a solid mass of cells. | It is a hollow structure |
| No cavity is found in the morula. | Cavity is found in blastocyst. |
| The cells are mostly undifferentiated and are of equal size. | Cells becomes differentiated into trophoblast and inner cell mass. |

**Q.5 What are the main structures you observe in TS of blastula?** NCERT

**Ans** The main structures seen in the slide showing TS of blastula are as follows:

(i) Cavity of blastocyst (blastocoel)
(ii) Trophoblast
(iii) Zona pellucida
(iv) Inner cell mass

**Q.6 Match the stages in column I with features in column II.** NCERT

| Column I | | Column II | |
|---|---|---|---|
| (a) | Trophoblast | (i) | Dividing cells of the morula |
| (b) | Morula | (ii) | Outer layer of blastula |
| (c) | Blastocoel | (iii) | Solid ball of cells |
| | | (iv) | Cavity |

**Ans** (a)-ii, (b)-iii, (c)-iv.

**Q.7 The sex cells in mammals, i.e. sperm and ova unite to form the zygote. What would be the ploidy of this zygote cell?**

**Ans** Sperm and ova are haploid ($n$) cells. They unite to form zygote which is a diploid ($2n$) structure.

**Q.8 What is the significance of cleavage?**

**Ans** The cleavage results into large number of newly formed cells (blastomeres). It lays foundation for the growth and development of the offspring's body.

**Q.9 When a female is considered to be pregnant?**

**Ans** A female is said to be pregnant when a fertilised egg implants itself in the uterus lining.

**Q.10 Differentiate between cleavage and a typical mitotic division.**

**Ans** Differences between cleavage and a typical mitotic division are as follows

| Cleavage | Mitotic division |
|---|---|
| It occurs in zygote | It occurs in the somatic cells. |
| Interphase is too short. | Interphase is long. |
| Size of blastomeres decreases as their number increase. | Size of daughter cells remains same. |

# Experiment 6.a

## AIM

To study Mendelian inheritance (Law of segregation) using seeds of different colour/sizes of any plant.

## Theory/Principle

**Genetics** is a branch of science which deals with the study of inheritance and variation of characters from parents to offsprings. **Gregor Johann Mendel**, also known as the **Father of Genetics**, had conducted several hybridisation experiments on garden pea (*Pisum sativum*) for several years and proposed three different laws of inheritance based on his experiment.

### Mendel's Laws of Inheritance

The three laws of inheritance as proposed by Mendel are as follows:

**Law of Dominance** According to this law, out of two alleles present in heterozygous condition, only one is able to express its effect in the individual and that allele is called **dominant allele**. The other allele which does not express itself is called **recessive allele**, e.g. T (representing tallness) is dominant over t (representing dwarfness) in a pea plant. Therefore, T is the dominant allele and t is the recessive allele.

**Law of Segregation** Mendel hypothesised that allele pairs separate or segregate from each other at the time of gamete formation and the paired condition is restored by the random fusion of gametes, i.e. egg cell and sperm cell during fertilisation. So, gametes are pure for a character. This is the reason it is also called as **law of purity of gametes**. This law can be understood with the help of cross given.

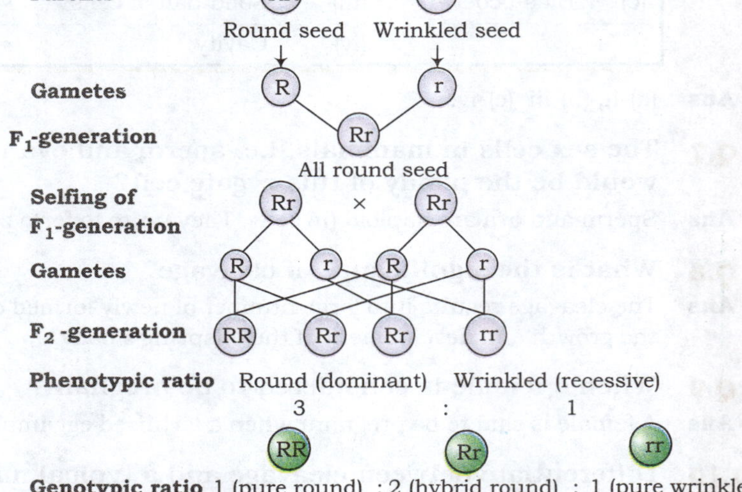


**Law of Independent Assortment** Mendel also found that each pair of alleles segregate independent of the other pairs of alleles during gamete formation.

## Requirements

Pea seed sample, plastic beakers, petridish, napkin, notebook, pencil/pen.

## Procedure

The students are to work in pairs and the given steps should be followed sequentially.

1. Take 64 round seeds in one beaker and 64 wrinkled seeds in the other to represent male and female gamete, respectively. Let the round seed be indicated by 'R' and wrinkled seed by 'r'.

2. Take a seed from each beaker and place them together (it represents fertilisation) on the napkin.
3. Just like the previous step, continue to pick seeds and arrange them in pairs. Thus, 64 pairs of seeds are obtained representing the 64 heterozygous $F_1$-progeny.
4. Note that all $F_1$-individuals are represented by one round and one wrinkled seed.
5. Put 32 $F_1$-progeny in one petridish and the remaining 32 in another petridish (representing the $F_1$ males and females).
6. Stir the seeds of each petridish with a pencil/pen for about 10 times taking care that no seed falls off.
7. To obtain $F_2$-generation, one student would withdraw one seed from one beaker labelled male and one from the other beaker labelled female, while keeping his/her eyes closed (to ensure randomness), and put them together in the stretched palm of the partner, who will put them together on the napkin spread over the table. Continue this process till all the seeds are paired. Thus, 64 offsprings of $F_2$ are obtained.
8. Note the genotype RR or Rr or rr of each pair and their possible phenotype.
9. Repeat the experiment (steps 1 to 8) for five more times with partners changing their roles. Pool all the data from the six repeats together.
10. Calculate the genotypic and phenotypic ratios of your pooled data.

## Observations

Record the result in the following table:

| Generation | Repeat No. | Total no. of individuals | Genotype(s) RR Rr rr | Phenotype(s) |
|---|---|---|---|---|
| $F_1$ | 1. | | | |
| | 2. | | | |
| | 3. | | | |
| | 4. | | | |
| | 5. | | | |
| | 6. | | | |
| | | Total | | |
| $F_2$ | 1. | | | |
| | 2. | | | |
| | 3. | | | |
| | 4. | | | |
| | 5. | | | |
| | 6. | | | |
| | | Total | | |

Phenotypic Ratio: in $F_1$.........
in $F_2$.........

Genotypic Ratio: in $F_1$.........
in $F_2$.........

## Result/Conclusion

The ratio of 3 : 1 in the $F_2$ suggests that in the $F_1$ heterozygotes, the recessive allele does not get destroyed and remains only in the recessive (dormant) state to get an opportunity to express itself when it has separated from the influence of the dominant allele.

- *Large sample of seeds (traits with shape) should be collected to minimise the error.*
- *The contrasting form of the trait should be observed carefully.*

## Viva-Voce

**Q.1 Who is known as the Father of Genetics? Name the plant on which he performed his experiments.**

**Ans** Gregor Johann Mendel, an Austrian monk, is known as the **Father of Genetics**. He performed his experiment on garden pea or *Pisum sativum*.

**Q.2 Give the genotypic ratio obtained in the monohybrid cross.**

**Ans** The genotypic ratio obtained in the monohybrid cross is 1:2:1 for $F_2$-generation.

**Q.3 Explain the observations on which the law of segregation is based.**

**Ans** Law of segregation is based on the following observations:

(i) The alleles do not show any blending.

(ii) Both the characters are recovered as such in $F_2$-generation though one of these is not seen in the $F_1$ stage.

**Q.4 What is hybrid?**

**Ans** Hybrid is an individual obtained from the crossing of two individuals that differ in atleast one pair of contrasting trait.

**Q.5 The round seeds obtained from a pea plant were sown in the ground. After few days, it was noted that the some pea plant bore wrinkled seeds, besides round seeds. What does this observation prove?**

**Ans** When round seed pea plant is sown, it also produces wrinkled seeds in its progeny because round seeds were hybrid and round shape of seed was dominant over wrinkled seed which gets segregated in $F_2$-generation.

**Q.6 Why did Mendel choose the pea plant for his experiment?**

**Ans** Mendel selected the pea plant because:

(i) Pea plant has several pairs of contrasting characters.

(ii) Pea plant has shorter life cycle.

(iii) These can be pollinated (self or cross) easily whenever required.

**Q.7 What is the difference between phenotype and genotype?**

**Ans** Phenotype is the visible expression or morphological appearance of an individual due to a particular genotype, while genotype is the genetic constitution of an organism.

**Q.8 Do you expect the same results in the terms of 3 : 1 ratio in $F_2$ if you had started with smaller number of beads (say 10 beads)?** NCERT

**Ans** No, the same ratio of 3 : 1 in $F_2$-generation will not be obtained in a smaller number of seeds or samples because the sample size is very small and there will be larger chances of errors in the experiment. To avoid the error possibilities large sample size should be taken.

# Experiment 6.b

## AIM

To study the Mendel's law of independent assortment.

## Theory/Principle

According to the law of independent assortment, when two pairs of traits are combined in a hybrid, segregation of one pair of characters is independent of the other pair of characters at the time of gamete formation.

Law of independent assortment involves random rearrangement of gene pairs in the offspring that results in both parental and new combination of characters. The genes of two different traits assort independently to give a probability ratio equal to segregation probability ratio of one allele pair multiply by segregation probability ratio of other allele pair which becomes $(3:1) \times (3:1) = 9:3:3:1$.

The law of independent assortment can be understood using the given dihybrid cross.

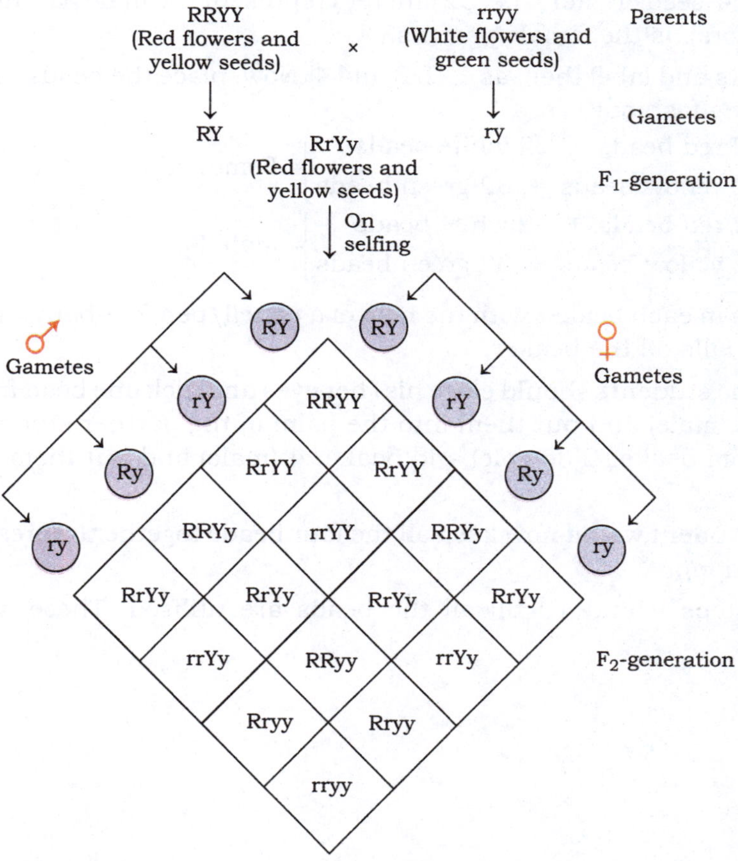


**Phenotypic ratio** = Red flowers and yellow seeds : Red flowers and green seeds : White flowers and yellow seeds : White flowers and green seeds = 9 : 3 : 3 : 1

**Genotypic ratio** = 1 : 2 : 2 : 4 : 1 : 2 : 1 : 2 : 1

## Requirements

Plastic beakers, 64 plastic beads each of yellow, green, red and white, to represent yellow and green colour of seed coat and red and white flowers respectively, napkin, notebook, pencil/pen.

## Procedure

The students are to work in pairs and the given steps should be followed sequentially.

1. Take 64 beads of each colour, i.e. yellow, green, red and white in four separate beakers.
2. Place the beakers containing yellow and red beads on your left side and those containing green and white beads on your right side. Here, the beakers on the left side represent plants bearing yellow seed and red flower (dominant characters YY, RR) and the beakers on the right side represent plants bearing green seeds and white flowers (recessive characters yy, rr).
3. Stir the beads in each beaker with a pencil/pen for about 5 minutes. Each bead represents alleles in the male and female gametes.
4. Pick up one bead from each beaker and put them together (represents fertilisation) on the napkin spread on the table.
5. Repeat the step number 4 till all the beads are utilised and 64 such 4-bead clusters are obtained. These clusters represent the $F_1$-generation. As certain their genotype and phenotype.
6. Let half of the 4-seed clusters, i.e. 32 clusters represent the male parents and the remaining half (32 clusters) as the female parents.
7. Take 4 beakers and label them as 1, 2, 3 and 4. Now, place the beads in each of the beakers in the following fashion:

   Beaker 1 : 32 red beads + 32 white beads
   Beaker 2 : 32 yellow beads + 32 green beads } Female $F_1$

   Beaker 3 : 32 red beads + 32 white beads
   Beaker 4 : 32 yellow beads + 32 green beads } Male $F_1$

8. Stir the beads in each beaker with the help of a pencil/pen for about 5 minutes, taking care that no bead falls off the beaker.
9. Now, one of the students should close his/her eyes and pick one bead from beaker 1 (female) and beaker 3 (male) and put them into the palm of the partner student. Similarly, pick a bead each from beaker 2 (female) and beaker 4 (male) and put them into the palm of the patner.
10. The partner student would now keep all the four beads together (representing $F_2$ individual after fertilisation).
11. Repeat the steps 9 and 10 till all the beads are utilised. These will represent 64 $F_2$ individuals.

12. Determine the genotype and phenotype of each of the 64 $F_2$-individuals and write down the number of individuals of different genotypes and phenotypes in the tabular form, remembering that Y (yellow seed colour) is dominant over y (green seed) and R (red flower) is dominant over r (white flower).
13. Repeat the whole procedure (steps 1 to 12) six times and tabulate your results.

## Observations

The symbol (–) indicates the presence of corresponding dominant or recessive allele.

Summarise the result (adding together the data of all the six repeats)

### $F_1$-generation

1. Total number of individuals ____________
2. Phenotype(s) ____________
3. Genotype(s) ____________

| Generation and repeat No. | Total No. of offsprings | Genotype | | | | Phenotype | | | |
|---|---|---|---|---|---|---|---|---|---|
| | | YYRR | YYrr | yyRR | yyrr | Yellow red | Yellow white | Green red | Green white |
| $F_1$ | | | | | | | | | |
| 1. | | | | | | | | | |
| 2. | | | | | | | | | |
| 3. | | | | | | | | | |
| 4. | | | | | | | | | |
| 5. | | | | | | | | | |
| 6. | | | | | | | | | |
| **Total** | | | | | | | | | |
| $F_2$ | | | | | | | | | |
| 1. | | | | | | | | | |
| 2. | | | | | | | | | |
| 3. | | | | | | | | | |
| 4. | | | | | | | | | |
| 5. | | | | | | | | | |
| 6. | | | | | | | | | |
| **Total** | | | | | | | | | |
| | | | | | | | | | |

### $F_2$-generation

1. Total number of individuals ________________
2. Phenotypes ________________
3. Number of individuals in each phenotypic class:

| Number | Phenotype |
|---|---|
| ________ | ________ |
| ________ | ________ |
| ________ | ________ |
| ________ | ________ |

4. Phenotypic ratio ________________
5. Genotypic ratio ________________
6. Number of individuals of each genotypic class:

| Number | Genotype |
|---|---|
| ________ | ________ |
| ________ | ________ |
| ________ | ________ |
| ________ | ________ |

7. Genotypic ratio ________________________

### Result/Conclusion

The four phenotypic classes in the $F_2$-generation are in ratio of 9 : 3 : 3 : 1 as expected from the law of independent assortment. The genotypic ratio would be (1 : 2 : 4 : 2) : (2 : 1) : (2 : 1) : 1.

**PRECAUTIONS**

- *Large sample of beads should be collected.*
- *Care should be taken while counting beads, so that any bead should not be missed, repeated or confused.*
- *The contrasting form of the trait should be observed carefully.*

# Viva-Voce

**Q.1 On which observation Mendel's law of independent assortment is based?**

**Ans** The law of independent assortment is based on the observation of dihybrid crosses.

**Q.2 Identify the following as gametes or individual. Tt, T, y, Aa, YyRr, XYZ, YYrr:**

**Ans** Gametes : T, y, XYZ. Individuals : Tt, Aa, YyRr, YYrr.

**Q.3 Give the phenotypic ratio for the law of independent assortment.**

**Ans** The phenotypic ratio for the law of independent assortment is 9 : 3 : 3 : 1.

**Q.4 How is independent assortment of alleles important from the point of view of variation?** NCERT

**Ans** Independent assortment means the random distribution of maternal and paternal genes to the gametes. It gives an idea that how one pair of homologous chromosomes separates into gametes and does not affect the separation of other pair. It explains that each gamete may have different combination of chromosomes which forms the basis of variation.

**Q.5 Linked traits fail to assort independently. Explain.** NCERT

**Ans** The genes that are located physically apart on non-homologous chromosomes assort independently. The segregation of alleles into gametes is influenced by linkage in which genes are located physically close to each other on the same chromosome and are more likely to be inherited as a pair.

**Q.6 If you are given a tall plant, how can you find out its genotype? Explain.**

**Ans** The genotype of a tall plant can be tested by a test cross, i.e. the cross between the given plant and its homozygous recessive counterpart. The homozygous tall (TT) plant will produce all tall plants, while the heterozygous tall (Tt) plant will produce both tall and dwarf plants in the ratio of 1 : 1.

# Experiment 7

## AIM

To study prepared pedigree charts of the genetic traits such as rolling of tongue, blood groups, ear lobes, widow's peak and colour blindness.

## Theory/Principle

The principle of inheritance of traits, given by Mendel is applicable to plants, animals and human beings. Control crosses to study inheritance that can be performed in plant or some other organisms, are not possible in case of human beings. Hence, study of the family history about inheritance of a particular trait provides an alternative. Such an analysis of traits in several generations of a family is called the **pedigree analysis**.

Pedigree is a diagram that shows occurrence and appearance of inherited traits in several generations of a family. It helps us to predict how traits or genetic conditions are passed down from one generation to the next.

Few internationally approved symbols used in this analytical study are as follows:

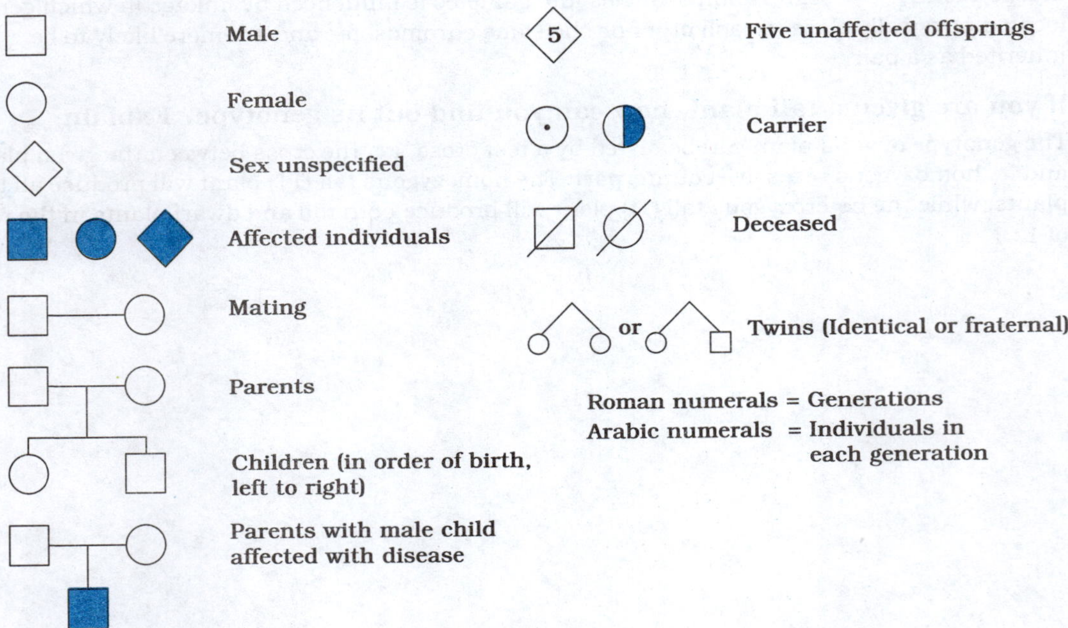


**Fig. 7.1** Symbols used for preparation of pedigree chart

The analysis of information from a pedigree makes it possible to determine how certain alleles are inherited, whether they are dominant or recessive and autosomal or sex-linked. The information regarding different types of genetic traits is given in the table below.

**Pedigree Chart Traits**

| S. No. | Type | Explanation | Traits |
|---|---|---|---|
| 1. | Autosomal dominant traits | Encoding gene present on any one of the autosomes and wild-type allele is recessive to its mutant allele. Mutant allele is dominant. | Rolling of tongue, widow's peak, brachydactyly, polydactyly, dimple in cheeks. |
| | **Males and females are equally affected.** | | |
| 2. | Autosomal recessive traits. | The mutant allele of a trait is recessive to its wild-type allele | Attached earlobe, albinism |
| | **Males and females are equally affected.** | | |
| 3. | X-linked dominant traits. (A rare trait.) | Encoding gene is present on X-chromosome and the mutant allele is dominant over its wild-type allele. | Incontinentia pigmenti |
| 4. | X-linked recessive traits. | Encoding gene is present on X-chromosome and its mutant allele is recessive to its wild-type allele. | Colour blindness, haemophilia. |
| | **Males express it even if they are hemizygous and females express the trait only when they are homozygous. Affected persons are related to one another through the maternal side of their family.** | | |
| 5. | Y-linked traits. | Encoding gene is present on Y-chromosome. It is present in all males. | Presence of hair on pinna (hypertrichosis) |
| | **Only in males.** | | |

## Requirements

Pedigree chart of a family with genetic disorder for more than one generation, paper and pencil.

## Procedure

1. Select the pedigree chart of a family with genetic disorder for more than one generation.
2. Observe it carefully and draw it in your notebook.
3. Write the appropriate comments in your file.

## Observations

### 1. Widow's Peak

It is a 'V'-shaped hairline across the forehead. It is a dominant trait. Thus, both homozygous dominant (AA) and heterozygous (Aa) individuals have widow's peak, while homozygous recessive (aa) individuals have a straight hairline.

**Fig. 7.2** Widow's peak trait

Pedigree chart of widow's peak

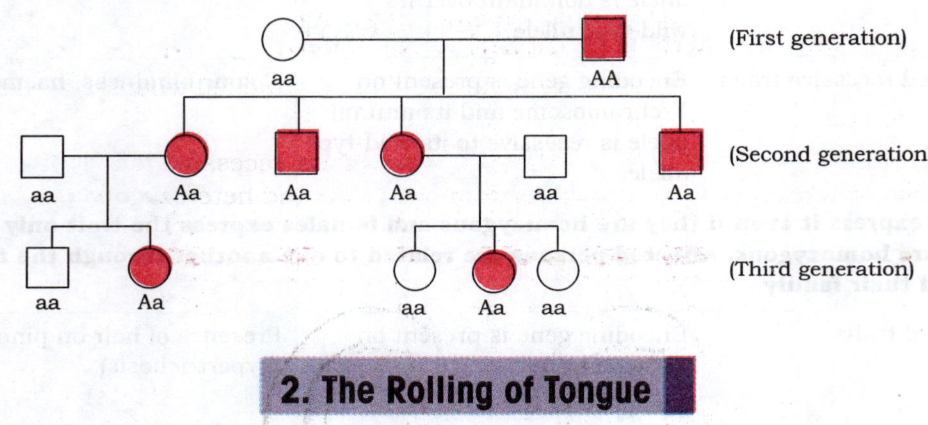


### 2. The Rolling of Tongue

Some people are able to roll their tongue in U-shape, while some are unable to do so. The inability to roll the tongue is caused by an autosomal recessive allele 'a'. Thus, both homozygous dominant (AA) and heterozygous (Aa) individuals are able to roll the tongue, while homozygous recessive (aa) individuals are unable to roll their tongue in this way.

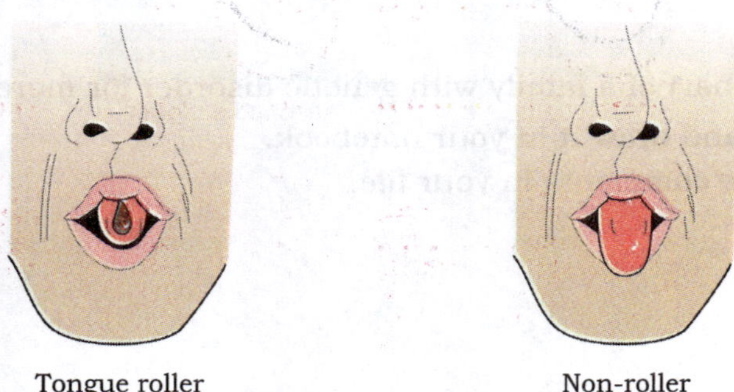


**Fig. 7.3** Tongue rolling trait

**Pedigree chart of rolling of tongue**

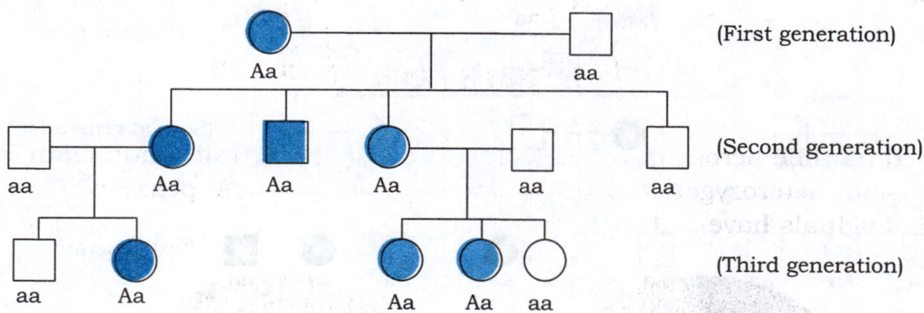


**Comments**

The given pedigree of widow's peak and rolling of tongue represents autosomal dominant trait. The characteristic features of inheritance of such type of traits are as follows.

(a) Transmission of traits occurs from parents of either sex.

(b) Both male and female offsprings are equally affected.

(c) The trait is present in each generation, i.e. the pedigree chart is vertical.

(d) Multiple generations are characteristically affected.

## 3. Attached Ear Lobes

Ear lobes that are connected directly to the head are said to be attached whereas those that hang below the point of attachment are said to be free.

The attached earlobe is a recessive trait. Thus, homozygous recessive (aa) individuals have attached ear lobes, whereas, both homozygous dominant (AA) and heterozygous (Aa) individuals have free ear lobes.

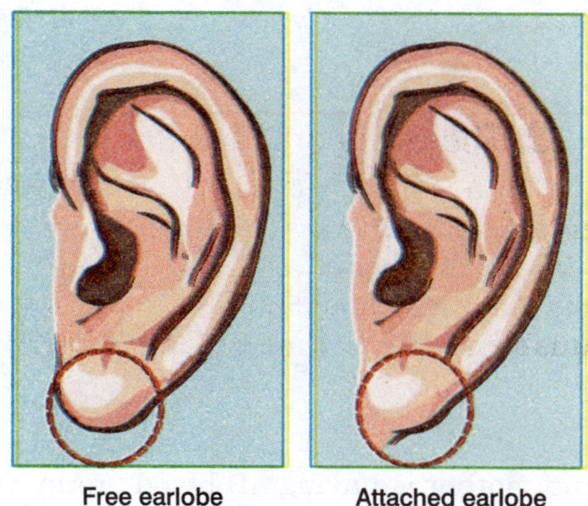


**Fig. 7.4** Ear lobes trait

**Pedigree chart of attached ear lobes**

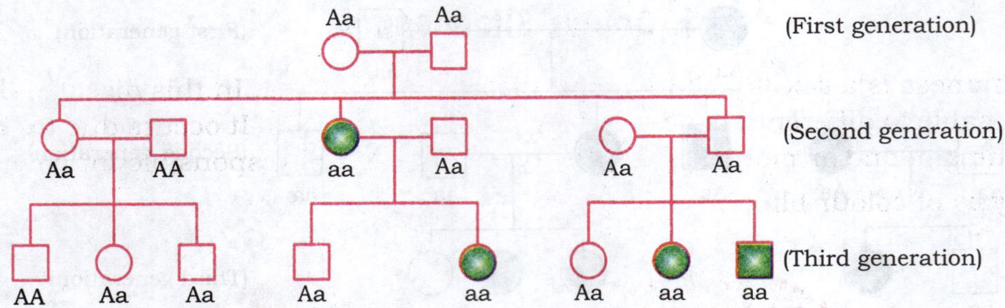


**Comments**

The given pedigree represents autosomal recessive trait. The characteristic features of inheritance of such type of trait is as follows

(a) These traits occurs in equal proportion in male and female siblings, whose parents are carries of the allele.

(b) The siblings are homozygous for the defective allele, but their parents though some may appear normal, are obviously heterozygous.

(c) Consanguinity may result in the appearance of such traits.

## 4. Blood Groups

In humans there are four types of blood groups i.e. A, B, AB and O. These blood groups are controlled by gene I. The gene I has three alleles $I^A, I^B$ *and* $I^O$.

Alleles $I^A$ and $I^B$ are dominant over $I^O$ and $I^A$ and $I^B$ are co-dominant over each other.

Pedigree chart of blood groups

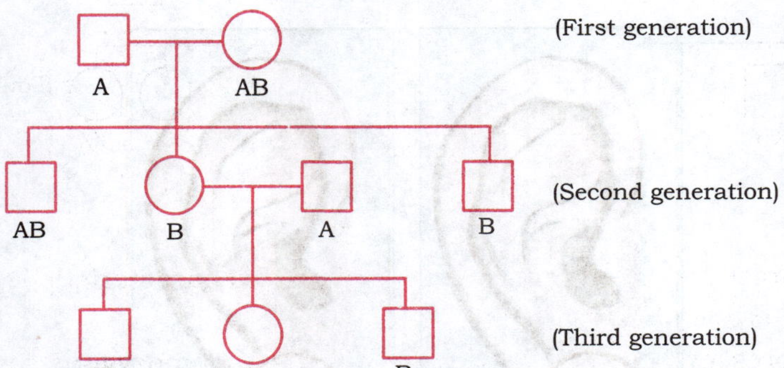


**Comments**

1. The father is having A and mother is having AB blood group, respectively.
2. The children of such parents may have blood group A, B or AB.
3. In third generation, the children may have A, B, AB or O blood group as parents are heterozygous for blood group A ($I^AI^O$) and B ($I^BI^O$). They can pass on the allele $I^AI^O$ (A blood group), $I^BI^O$ (B), $I^AI^B$ (AB) or $I^OI^O$ (O) to their offsprings.

## 5. Colour Blindness

The colour blindness is a sex-linked recessive disorder of humans. In this disease, the affected individual is unable to differentiate between red and green colours. It occurs due to the absence or malfunctioning of one or more of the three types of cone cell responsible for colour vision.

Pedigree analysis of colour blindness

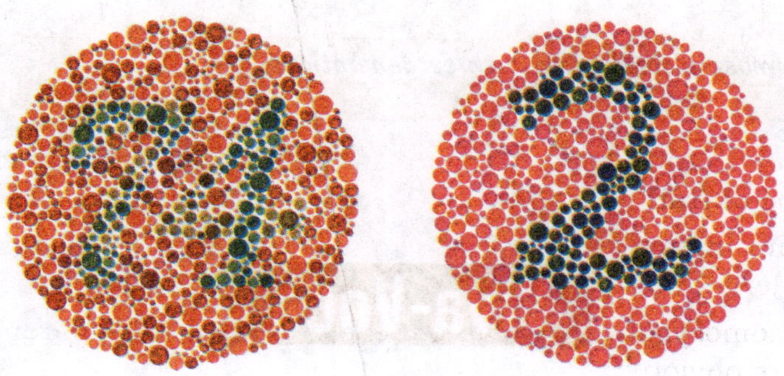

**Pedigree chart of colour blindness**

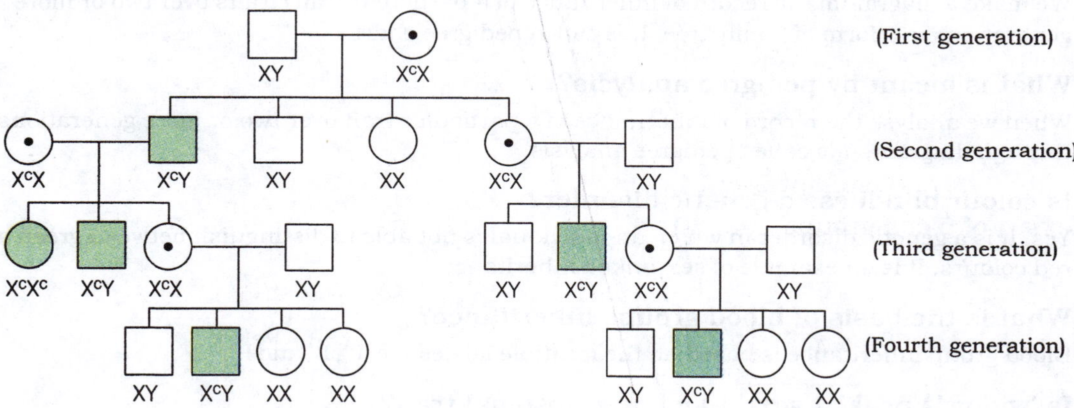


**Comments**

The given pedigree represents sex-linked recesive trait. The characteristic feature of inheritance of such type of traits are as follows.

(a) The females expresses the trait only when they are homozygous for the mutant allele whereas, males does so even when they are hemizygous for it.

(b) About half of the sons of the carrier (heterozygous for the trait) females are affected.

(c) In case of homozygous females showing the trait, 50% of her daughters and all of her sons are likely to be affected. Therefore, it can be concluded that males are most affected population in this category.

(d) Affected persons are related to one another through the maternal side of their family.

(e) Any evidence of male to male transmission of the trait rules out the X-linked inheritance.

## Result/Conclusion

After careful study of a pedigree chart, it is possible to conclude whether a trait is dominant or recessive and whether it is an autosomal or sex-linked trait.

### PRECAUTIONS

- *The prior knowledge of genetic disorder is must to identify the presence of a particular disorder in pedigree analysis.*
- *The pedigree chart must include atleast three generations.*

## Viva-Voce

**Q.1 How do we study inheritance of a character in a family?**

**Ans** We make a diagrammatic record of inheritance of a particular trait/traits over two or more generations in a form of family tree. It is called pedigree chart.

**Q.2 What is meant by pedigree analysis?**

**Ans** When we analyse the record of inheritance of a particular trait over two or more generations through diagram, it is called pedigree analysis.

**Q.3 Is colour blindness a genetic disorder?**

**Ans** Yes, it is a genetic disorder in which an individual is not able to distinguish between green and red colours. It is an example of sex-linked inheritance.

**Q.4 What is the basis of blood groups inheritance?**

**Ans** Blood group inheritance is based on the multiple alleles, i.e. $I^A$, $I^O$ and $I^B$.

**Q.5 Is 'widow's peak' a sex-linked or autosomal trait?**

**Ans** It is an autosomal dominant trait.

**Q.6 Who discovered blood groups?**

**Ans** Landsteiner discovered the blood groups A, B, AB and O.

**Q.7 How does pedigree analysis help in genetic studies?**

**Ans** It helps in knowing the possibilities of the presence of a trait in homozygous or heterozygous state in a particular offspring. It gives the probability that a certain genetic disorder may be passed on to the offspring from parents, having the disorder in their family history.

**Q.8 What does the horizontal line represent in a pedigree chart?**

**Ans** The horizontal line in a pedigree represents marriage or mating between two individuals.

**Q.9 What does ⊡ sign represent?**

**Ans** It means the individual is male and is a carrier of disease, i.e. it is a heterozygous carrier individual.

**Q.10 Discuss the differences in the patterns of autosome linked recessive and sex chromosome linked pedigree.** NCERT

**Ans** In an autosomal recessive pedigree, the parents are usually normal but carriers and the trait's appears equally among male and female siblings who are homozygous for defective allele. In a sex-linked (X-linked) recessive pedigree, females express the trait when they are homozygous, while males express it even in heterozygous state.

**Q.11 How will you differentiate between autosome linked dominant and sex chromosome linked dominant pedigree chart? Explain.** NCERT

**Ans** In an autosomal dominant pedigree, both males and females are equally affected, and the traits appears in each generation showing vertical pattern of inheritance. In a sex-linked dominant pedigree if a males is affected, all of his daughters and none of his sons will be affected.

**Q.12 Can a gene present on Y-chromosome express its trait in female?**

**Ans** No, a gene present on Y-chromosome cannot express its trait in females due to absence of Y-chromosome in female.

**Q.13 Can certain hereditary diseases be prevented?**

**Ans** Yes, certain hereditary diseases can be prevented by careful study of the trait using pedigree.

**Q.14 If a gene is present on an autosome, is it more likely to affect male or female offspring?**

**Ans** If a gene is present on an autosome, it is equally likely to affect both male and female offspring.

# Experiment 8

## AIM

To study emasculation, bagging and tagging by trying out an exercise on controlled pollination.

## Theory/Principle

Plant breeding is a science of improving the traits of plants to produce new varieties which are far better than the original type. To achieve this, plant breeders use the technique of **artificial hybridisation** in crop improvement programmes.

The various steps involved in plant breeding programme are as follows:

1. Collection of germplasm/genetic variability.
2. Selection of parents with desired characteristics.
3. Cross hybridisation among selected parents.
4. Selection and testing of new superior recombinants.
5. Testing, release and commercialisation of new cultivar.

Controlled pollination is done to direct plant breeding for desired traits. There are three methods involved in the process of controlled pollination, which are given below.

### Emasculation

In this process, stamens or anthers are removed from a bisexual flower before anther dehiscence, without affecting female reproductive organs, to avoid self-pollination.

Based on the size of flowers, emasculation can be done in two different ways.

(i) **Scissors/Forcep Method** This method is adopted for plants having large size flowers, e.g. cotton, pea.

(ii) **Hot Water Method** This method is adapted for plants having small size flowers, e.g. paddy, *Sorghum*.

***Note*** *This step of emasculation is only needed when the flowers under study are bisexual. If the female parent produces unisexual flowers, then this step is not needed.*

### Bagging

The emasculated flower is immediately enclosed in a bag made of butter paper or polythene to avoid pollination by unwanted pollen. This process is called bagging. In case of unisexual flowers, they are bagged before bloom.

### Tagging/Labelling

In this process, a tag is attached to the emasculated flower after pollination. The label includes the details such as the name of the parent plant, date of emasculation, date of controlled pollination, etc.

## Requirements

Ornamental plants/wild plants bearing large bisexual flowers, magnifying lens, tweezers, small sharp scissors, brush, alcohol, plastic bags, rubber bands, paper clips and tags.

## Procedure

(i) Select a plant bearing large bisexual flower in bud condition where anthesis has not occurred.

Gently open the bud and remove the stamens using small sharp scissors. Mark this as a female parent plant.

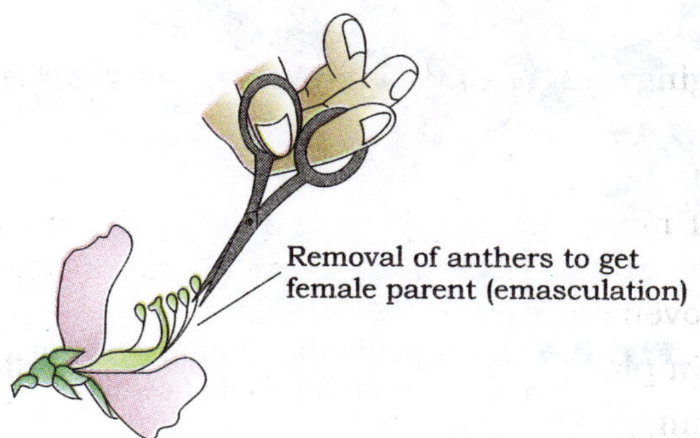


**Fig. 8.1** Scissors method of emasculation

### Alcohol/Hot Water Method of Emasculation

(i) This method is adopted for plants / crops with small sized flowers like paddy, *Sorghum*, etc.

(ii) The panicles of flowers are dipped in hot water for 10 minutes to kill anthers.

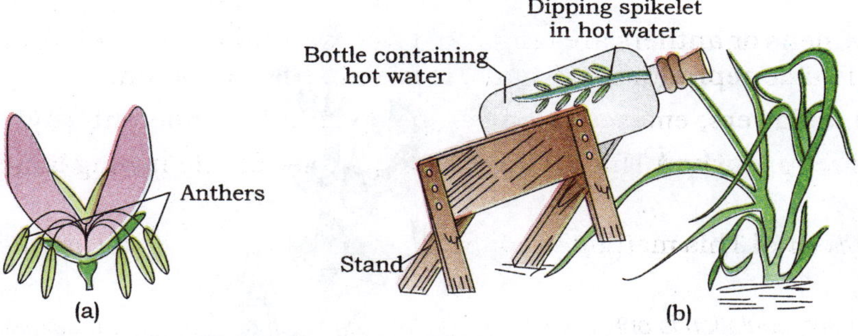


**Fig. 8.2** (a) Single spikelet of paddy (b) Method showing emasculation in experimental paddy plant by hot water

(ii) Cover the emasculated female flowers with transparent plastic bags (with minute holes in it) to avoid the undesired pollen from falling on it. The bag should be held securely in place with paper clip/rubber band.

(iii) The stigma of emasculated flower is dusted with desirable pollen grain through physical contact with the anthers of chosen male plant. Use a brush or tweezer if necessary, to dust the stigmatic surface with pollen.

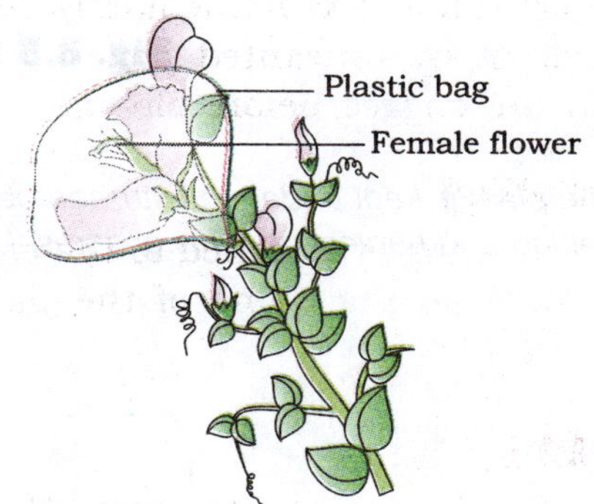


**Fig. 8.3** Bagging of an emasculated female flower

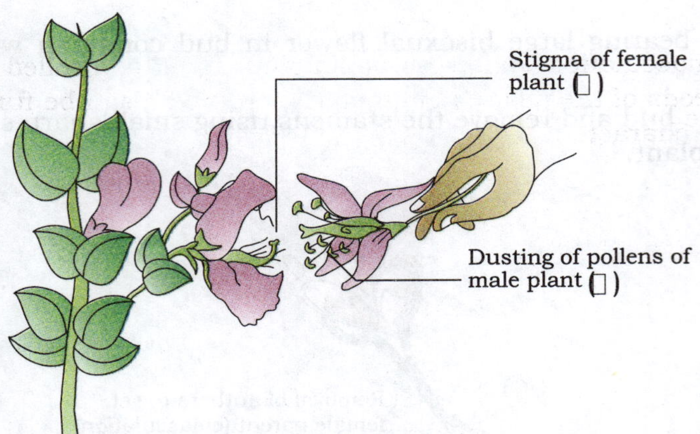


**Fig. 8.4** Cross-pollination being performed on emasculated female flower

(iv) Cover the pollinated flower again with the bag immediately.

(v) For easy identification, tag this plant and the tag must includes all necessary information about the experiment like plant variety of male and female parent, date of emasculation and pollination, etc.

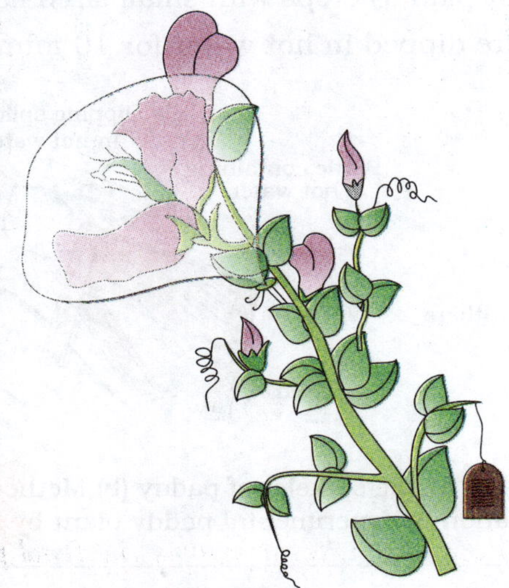

**Fig. 8.5** Plant showing labelled tag

***Note*** *The plant is kept under undisturbed observation and proper care of experimental plants is taken till seed setting and harvesting. This ensures the success of the experiment.*

## Result

By the process of emasculation and cross-pollination under controlled conditions, the female plant will produce seeds of the desired characteristics, which can be further grown to produce hybrids with desired characters.

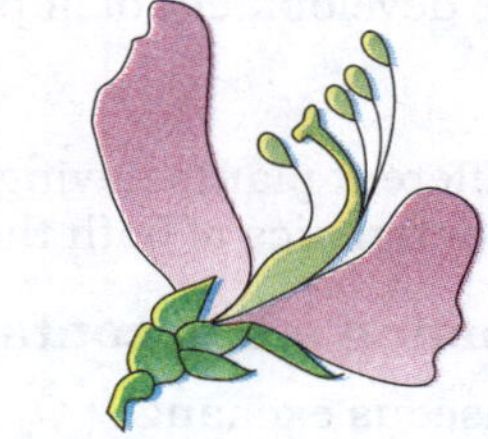

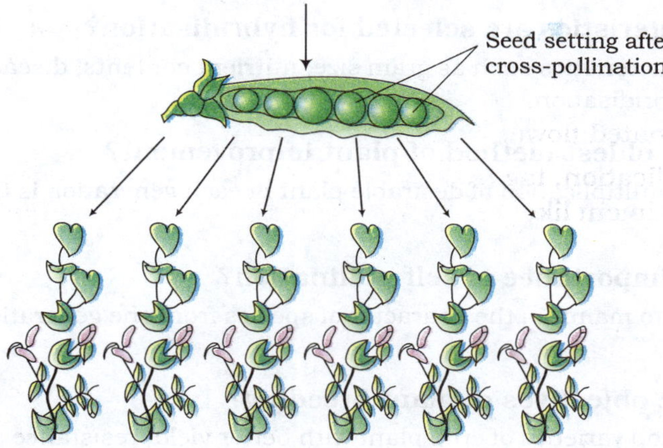


**Fig. 8.6** Seeds will show desired characters in the next generation of the plant

### PRECAUTIONS

- *Selected parents should be pure breeding and healthy.*
- *Emasculation should be done carefully, without injuring the floral parts.*
- *The emasculated flower should be bagged properly to prevent pollination with undesirable pollen.*
- *The interval between pollen collection and pollination should be minimised as pollen viability is only maintained for a short time period.*

## Viva-Voce

**Q.1 What is plant breeding?**

**Ans** It is a science which deals with the development of improved varieties of plants.

**Q.2 What is hybridisation?**

**Ans** It is a process of crossing of two different plants having desirable characters to get a superior variety which combines good characteristics of both the parents.

**Q.3 What are the advantages of using a bag containing minute pores?** NCERT

**Ans** The minute pores will allow the gaseous exchange ( $O_2$ and $CO_2$) needed by the plant but prevent the pollination by not allowing pollens to reach the female flowers.

**Q.4 What characteristics are selected for hybridisation?**

**Ans** Desirable characteristics such as grain size, nutrient contents, disease resistance, etc., are selected for hybridisation.

**Q.5 Which is the oldest method of plant improvement?**

**Ans** Selection and multiplication of desirable plant in each generation is the oldest method of plant improvement.

**Q.6 What is the importance of self-pollination?**

**Ans** It is important to maintain the character of species from one generation to other generation.

**Q.7 What are the objectives of plant breeding?**

**Ans** It aims to develop varieties of crop plant with better yield, resistance against disease and pests and tolerance in the prevailing climatic conditions.

**Q.8 Which process is better among self-pollination or cross-pollination and why?**

**Ans** Cross-pollination is better because it leads to the greater variability and recombination of characteristics of two different plants. This helps in the formation of new organism that have better adaptability.

**Q.9 Why do we need to test the new recombinants before releasing them in the commercial market?**

**Ans** It is done to select the superior hybrids and ensure that hybrid does not contain any harmful characters of any of the parent. The individual hybrids with only desired characters are selected and tested.

**Q.10 Why is emasculation performed before anthesis?** NCERT

**Ans** Emasculation is performed before anthesis to avoid self-pollination.

**Q.11 Should we discard self-pollination totally?**

**Ans** No, it is a natural process which maintains the uniformity in characters in successive generations, so we should not totally discard it.

# Experiment 9

## AIM

To identify common disease causing organisms like *Ascaris, Entamoeba, Plasmodium* and any fungus causing ringworms through permanent slides, models or virtual images or specimens. Comment on symptoms of the diseases that they cause.

## Theory/Principle

A disease is an abnormal condition that affects the body of an organism. A huge number of organisms cause diseases in humans and other organisms. These disease causing organisms are called **pathogens**. These organisms exihibit characteristic features in their external morphology. Pathogens are parasites which obtain the food of host from living organisms including humans and cause considerable damage to the body of host which can be fatal sometimes. After invading the human body, they cause characteristic symptoms of the disease which are specific in nature.

## Requirements

Permanent slides, models or virtual images or specimens of *Plasmodium, Entamoeba, Ascaris* and ringworm fungi *(Microsporum, Epidermophyton, Trichophyton,* etc.), a hand lens and a compound microscope.

## Procedure

1. Study the permanent slides under compound microscope or observe the models/virtual images/specimen.
2. Note down the identification characteristics of pathogens in the practical record book.
3. Draw labelled diagram of the pathogens observed.

## Observations

### *Entamoeba histolytica*

#### Classification

| | | |
|---|---|---|
| Phylum | – | Protozoa |
| Class | – | Rhizopoda |
| Genus | – | *Entamoeba* |
| Species | – | *histolytica* |

#### Characteristics

1. It is a unicellular organism, irregular in shape due to the presence of pseudopodia.
2. It has single big nucleus, placed eccentrically in the cell.
3. In the nucleus, there is a peripheral ring of nucleoprotein granules and a central karyosome, and the rest of the space appears empty.
4. The cell shows the presence of few food vacuoles, but contractile vacuoles are absent.
5. Few *Entamoeba* cells may show mature quadrinucleated cyst.

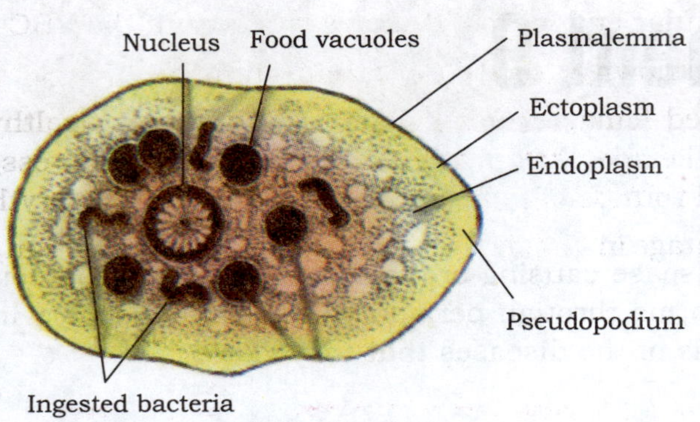


**Fig. 9.1** *Entamoeba histolytica*

## Interactions with Host

1. It is an endoparasite of human intestine and causes **amoebic dysentery** or **amoebiasis**.
2. Source of infection is through the contaminated food and water.
3. The parasite feeds on RBCs of the host by damaging the wall of large intestine and reaching the blood capillaries.
4. The amoebic cysts are present in the fecal matter of infected person. These can be seen on microscopic examination of stool.

## Symptoms

1. Person affected with *Entamoeba* complaints of severe abdominal pain and spasms.
2. Patient passes out loose, mucus filled watery stools. In severe cases, blood clots may also appear in the stools.
3. The presence of blood in stools indicates that ulcers have been caused in intestine by the pathogen.
4. The patient may have slightly enlarged liver with pain in the upper right portion of the abdomen.

# *Plasmodium vivax* (Malarial Parasite)

## Classification

| | | |
|---|---|---|
| Phylum | – | Protozoa |
| Class | – | Sporozoa |
| Genus | – | *Plasmodium* |
| Species | – | *vivax* |

## Characteristics

1. It is unicellular.
2. A big vacuole is present in the centre of cell and the cytoplasm is accumulated at one place containing the nucleus.
3. Signet ring stage is observed in the erythrocytes of affected individuals.

#### Interactions with Host

1. It is an intracellular endoparasite seen easily within the RBC of the infected person.
2. The protozoa is known to cause **malaria** in humans.
3. When an infected female *Anopheles* mosquito bites a healthy individual, it transfer the infective stage, i.e.sporozoites into the peripheral blood vessels. These sporozoites then undergo several rounds of multiplication in the liver and erythrocytes.
4. The signet ring stage in RBC is the diagnostic feature in human, infected with *Plasmodium.*

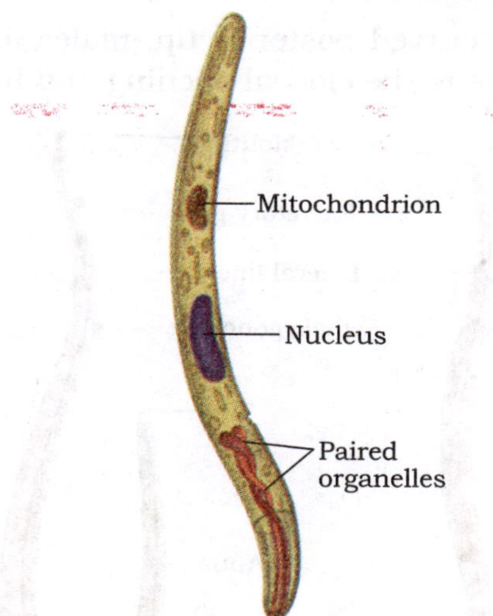


**Fig. 9.2** Spindle-shaped sporozoites of *Plasmodium*

#### Symptoms

1. The infected person suffers from headache, muscular pains and loss of appetite.
2. The person suffers from shivering and high fever with chills followed by profuse sweating at an interval of alternate days.
3. The temperature of body goes down to normal, till the next attack takes place after 48 hours.
4. Sleeplessness and restlessness accompanies along with all the above mentioned symptoms.

## *Ascaris lumbricoides* (Intestinal Roundworm)

#### Classification

| | | |
|---|---|---|
| Phylum | – | Aschelminthes |
| Class | – | Nematoda |
| Genus | – | *Ascaris* |
| Species | – | *lumbricoides* |

#### Characteristics

1. The body of *Ascaris* is long (20 to 40 cm), cylindrical (5 to 6 mm in diameter) with no segmentation.
2. The animal shows sexual dimorphism. The female is longer than male.

3. Both the ends are pointed, with the posterior end of male curved ventrally.
4. Single longitudinal lines are present on the dorsal, ventral and on the two lateral side throughout the body. However, the lateral lines are more distinct than other lines.
5. **Mouth** is present at the anterior end which is surrounded by three lips, one at mid-dorsal position and other two at ventro-lateral position (use magnifying glass to view them).
6. **Excretory pore** is present behind the anterior end on ventral surface.
7. In females, a **genital aperture** is present on the mid- ventral line at about one third of the distance from the anterior end.
8. In addition to the ventrally curved posterior tip, males also have two chitinous **penial spicules** which are very close to the cloacal opening and help in copulation.

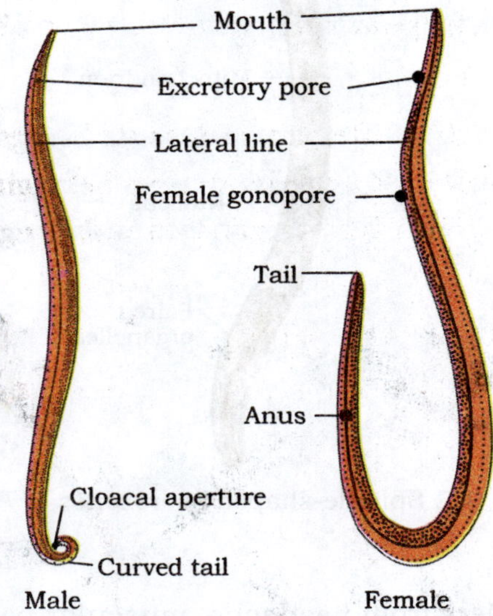


**Fig. 9.3** *Ascaris lumbricoides*

## Interaction with Host

*Ascaris* is an endoparasite of small intestine of human beings. The worm enters the host body by consumption of soil contaminated with its egg. It subsequently feeds on the host's semidigested food with the help of specialised structures.

## Symptoms

1. *Ascaris* worm infests a single host and obstructs the intestinal passage thereby causing abdominal discomforts.
2. The infected person complaints of colic pain.
3. The patients may also suffers from impaired digestion, vomiting and diarrhoea in severe infestation.
4. An infected person shows the symptoms of malnourishment like anaemia, retarded body growth and mental growth specially in children.
5. Person looses weight and feels tired and lethargic.

## Ringworm fungus

### Classification

| | | |
|---|---|---|
| Kingdom | – | Fungi |
| Class | – | Deuteromycetes |
| Genus | – | *Trichophyton* |
| Species | – | *rubrum* |

### Characteristics

1. The texture of the hyphae of fungus is waxy and glabrous to cotton-like.
2. Unstained hyphae are white, yellowish brown to reddish brown in colour.

### Interactions with Host

Ringworm fungus feeds on keratin of the skin of human beings.

1. The physical contact with infected persons, or their belongings may spread the infections.
2. Usually scissors and clips remain contaminated with fungal spores and cause infection in healthy persons.

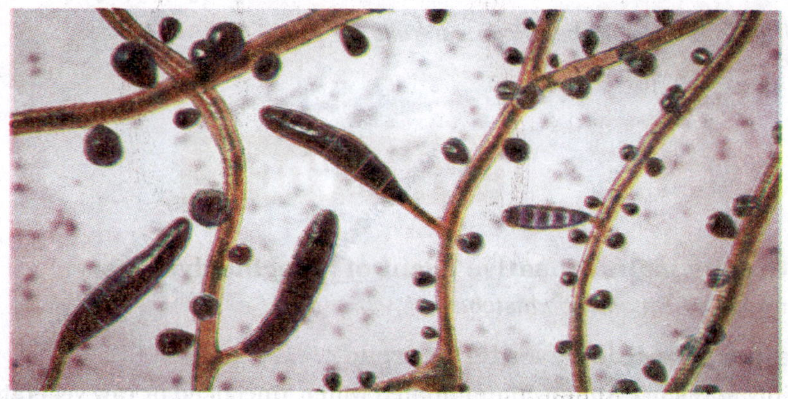

**Fig. 9.4** Conidia of ringworm fungi (*Trichophyton* sp.)

### Symptoms

1. **Symptoms on Scalp** Reddish or yellowish crust appears on scalp. Hair becomes lustless and grey. In severe cases, it leads to baldness.
2. **Symptoms on Skin** The infected area of skin is itchy, red, raised having scaly patches. It is more red on the periphery than in the centre creating a ring like appearance.
3. **Symptoms on Foot** It specially appears in between the toes because of the presence of moisture. A watery fluid leaks out from the infected areas. Cracking/ scaling of skin of foot occurs due to the severe infection.
4. **Symptoms on Nails** The nails show discolouration, become chalky and brittle.

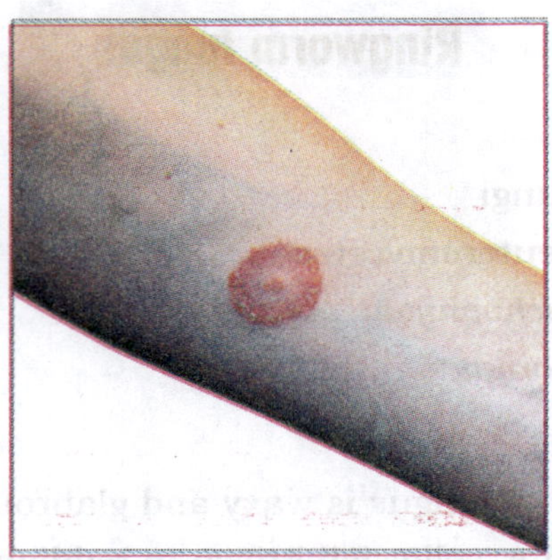

**Fig. 9.5** Person infected with ringworm showing lesion on hand

## PRECAUTIONS

- *The specimens should be examined carefully with naked eyes and with the help of hand lens.*
- *Make your observation first under low power followed by higher magnification.*
- *Labelled diagrams should be drawn carefully .*

# Viva-Voce

**Q.1 Identify the main causative agent of amoebic dysentery.**
**Ans** It is caused by *Entamoeba histolytica.*

**Q.2 How does amoebic dysentery spread?**
**Ans** It mainly spreads through contaminated water, uncooked or raw vegetables.

**Q.3 List the symptoms of malaria.**
**Ans** High fever with chills followed by profuse sweating at an interval of alternate days are the main symptoms of malaria.

**Q.4 What is ascariasis?**
**Ans** The manifestation of *Ascaris* infection in an individual's body is called ascariasis.

**Q.5 How does worm infection spread?**
**Ans** Infection of worms spreads mainly through the consumption of the cyst infested raw vegetables, contaminated water and soil, etc.

**Q.6 What are the symptoms caused by *Ascaris* infection?**
**Ans** Severe abdominal pain along with nutritional deficiency are the symptoms caused by *Ascaris* infection.

**Q.7 What is a ringworm?**

**Ans** Ringworm is a symptom of fungal infections on skin, scalp, nails, etc., caused by a group of fungi together known as dermatophytes.

**Q.8 Is ringworm contagious?**

**Ans** Yes, it spreads from diseased to healthy person by direct or indirect contact.

**Q.9 What is digenetic life cycle?**

**Ans** The completion of the life of parasitic organisms in two hosts is called digenetic life cycle, e.g. *Plasmodium* complete its life cycle in man and mosquito.

**Q.10 Name the sexual phase of *Plasmodium*.**

**Ans** The sexual phase of *Plasmodium* is gametogony.

**Q.11 List some measures to prevent malaria.**

**Ans** The breeding places of mosquito should be sprayed by insecticides and mosquito repellents and mosquito net should be used while sleeping.

**Q.12 What is the treatment for the ascariasis?**

**Ans** Anti-helminthic drugs are recommended to deworm the person as it kills the worms.

**Q.13 Name the infective stage of *Plasmodium* parasite?**

**Ans** The infective stage in *Plasmodium* parasite is called sporozoites.

**Q.14 What do you understand by incubation period?**

**Ans** It is the time period between the entry of pathogen in the host till the appearance of first symptom of its infection.

**Q.15 What is the incubation period in case of malaria caused by *P. vivax*.**

**Ans** It is typically 12 to 18 days.

**Q.16 Which stage of *Plasmodium* is called diagnostic stage?**

**Ans** Signet ring stage of *Plasmodium* is called diagnostic stage because *Plasmodium* takes round-shape inside the infected red blood cells.

**Q.17 How can we prevent the spread of ringworm infection?**

**Ans** Prevention of ringworm is done by following practices:

(i) Isolate the infected person.

(ii) Boil/sterilise the objects used by diseased person.

(iii) Maintain strict personal hygiene.

(iv) Keep infected areas dry and apply anti-fungal ointments.

# Experiment 10

## AIM

To study the symbiotic association (models/specimen) found in root nodules of leguminous plants, *Cuscuta* on host and lichens.

## Theory/Principle

In nature animals, plants and microbes interact with one another in various ways.

When two different species interact with each other (interspecific interaction) and are in close association in such a way that at least one species is benefited (positive impact) while the other species may have positive, negative or neutral impact, such association is called **symbiotic relationship**.

There are three basic types of symbiotic relationship

- **Mutualism** In this type of relationship both the species are benefited.
- **Commensalism** In this type of relationship only one species is benefited, while the other is neither benefited nor harmed.
- **Parasitism** In this type of relationship only one species is benefited, and the other is harmed. Generally the parasite does not kill the host.

## Requirements

Model/specimen showing symbiotic association in root nodules of leguminous plant (pea plant), *Cuscuta* on host and a lichen.

## Procedure

1. Observe the association between the *Rhizobium* bacterium and roots of leguminous plant, *Cuscuta* and its host and lichens with the help of model or specimen.
2. Note the special features of each specimen and draw a well labelled diagram.

## Observations

1. ***Rhizobium* in root nodules of leguminous plant (pea plant)**

   (i) *Rhizobium* bacteria are present in the root nodules of leguminous plant and forms a symbiotic relationship, i.e. mutualism.

   (ii) Rhizobia bacteria enter the leguminous plant through root hairs and forms an infection thread leading to development of nodule. The bacteria then convert the atmospheric nitrogen into ammonia that is used by the plant for its growth.

   (iii) In return, bacteria receive organic acids from the plant to use as a food source.

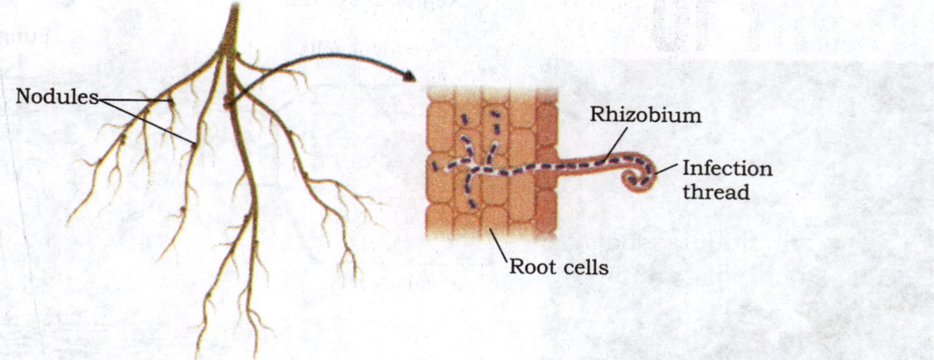


**Fig. 10.1** Roots of a leguminous plant infected with *Rhizobium*

2. ***Cuscuta* on Host**

(i) It is commonly called dodder or amarbel and live as stem ectoparasite (parasitism) on other plants.

(ii) It has scale-like leaves and lack chlorophyll.

(iii) Stem of *Cuscuta* is thin and slender-shaped. It winds around the stem of host plant and penetrates the host stem *via* **haustoria**.

(iv) Haustoria form direct connection to the vascular bundles of the host and withdraw water carbohydrates and other solutes.

(v) Roots of *Cuscuta* are temporary and die as soon as it makes connection with host plant.

(vi) *Cuscuta* can weaken or kill plant and reduce its crop yield.

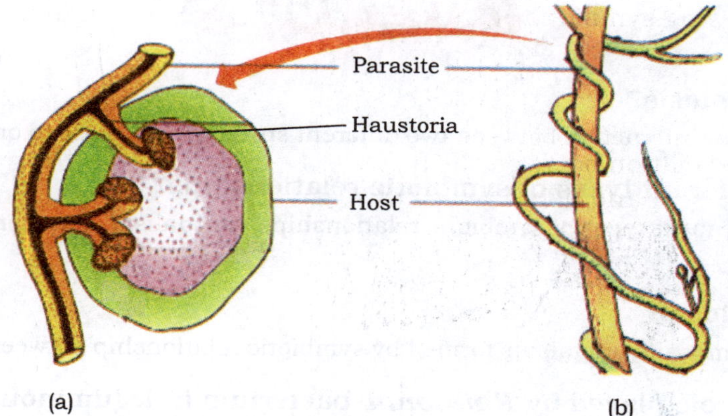


**Fig. 10.2** (a) T.S of host along with *Cuscuta*, (b) *Cuscuta* on the host

3. **Lichens**

(i) Lichens are composite organisms representing a symbiotic association (mutualism) between fungus and algae.

(ii) The algal component is known as **phycobiont** and fungal component is known as **mycobiont**.

(iii) Algae prepares food for fungi and in return fungi provide shelter and absorb mineral, nutrients and water for its partner.

(iv) Lichens can grow on lands, rocks, tree trunks and walls of houses.

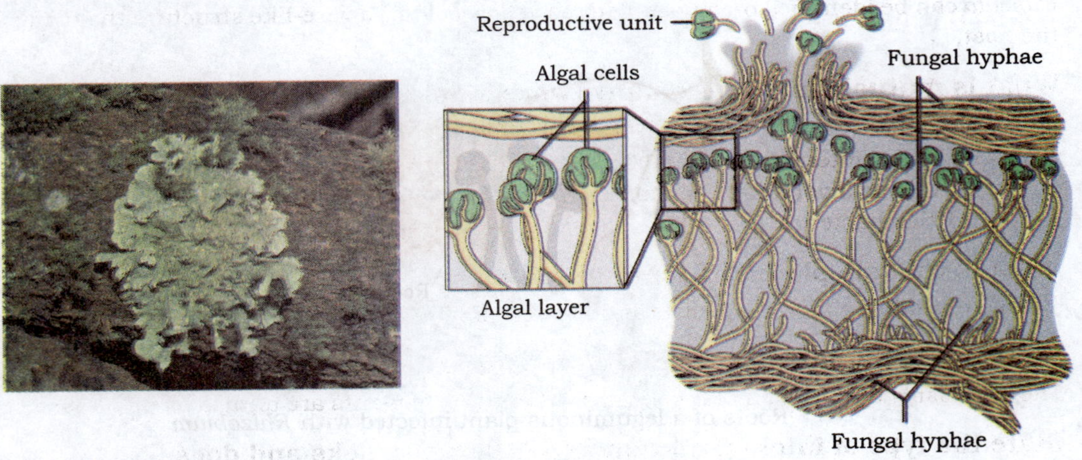


**Fig. 10.3** Lichen morphology

## PRECAUTIONS

- *The specimens should be carefully handled.*
- *The symbiotic features of plants should be noted.*

# Viva-Voce

**Q.1 What is symbiosis?**

**Ans** A relationship or interaction between two different species living close to one another.

**Q.2 What are different types of symbiotic relationships?**

**Ans** There are three main types of symbiotic relationships; mutualism, commensalism and parasitism.

**Q.3 What are lichens?**

**Ans** Lichens are composite organisms formed by symbiotic relationship between fungi and algae.

**Q.4 What is the role played by *Rhizobium* bacterium in leguminous plants?**

**Ans** The bacteria attach to the roots of leguminous plant and produce nodules. In these nodules rhizobia fix atmospheric nitrogen and convert it into ammonia that plant can use for its growth.

**Q.5 Give an example of parasitic symbiotic relationship.**

**Ans** *Cuscuta* and the host plant.

**Q.6 Where can you observe *Rhizobium* in leguminous plant?**

**Ans** *Rhizobium* are primarily observed in the root nodules of leguminous plant.

**Q.7 What is the function of haustoria?**

**Ans** Haustoria fixes the plant on host and helps to absorb nutrients from the host.

**Q.8 How can you identify *Cuscuta* on a host plant?**

**Ans** *Cuscuta* can be identified on a host plant as yellow coloured wire-like structure that wrap around the host.

**Q.9 What is mutualism? Mention any two examples where the organisms involved are commercially exploited in agriculture.**

**Ans** Mutualism is an interaction that confers benefit to both the interacting species. Two examples where organisms involved are commercially exploited in agriculture are mycorrhizal fungi and nitrogen fixing bacteria.

**Q.10 What is the role played by algae in symbiosis?**

**Ans** The algae performs photosynthesis and nitrogen fixation in symbiosis with fungi.

**Q.11 What are the organisms that feed on plant sap and other plant parts called?**

**Ans** The organisms that feed on plant sap and other parts of plants are termed as phytophagous.

**Q.12 State the type of interaction that exists between ticks and dogs.**

**Ans** Parasitism (ectoparasite).

**Q.13 Give the name of two parasitic plants and two parasitic animals.**

**Ans** Parasitic plants are *Cuscuta* and *Viscum* and parasitic animals are mites and lice.

**Q.14 An orchid plant is growing on the branch of mango tree. How do you describe this interaction between the orchid and mango tree?**

**Ans** Orchid is an epiphytic plant that grows on a branch of mango tree and they together show commensalism. In this interaction, orchid is benefited and the mango tree is neither harmed nor benefited at all.

**Q.15 Name the type of association that the genus-*Glomus* exhibits with higher plants.**

**Ans** The genus-Glomus forms mutualistic association with the roots of higher plants, known as mycorrhiza.

# Experiment 11

## AIM

Study of homologous and analogous organs in plants and animals with the help of flash cards/ models.

## Theory/Principle

Comparative anatomical and morphological evidences show the similarities and differences among the present-day organisms and those that existed years ago. These similarities can be interpreted to understand whether common ancestors were shared or not. The common ancestory between different organisms can be determined by homology and analogy.

### Homologous Organs and Homology

The organs that have same origin and anatomy, but are different in appearance and perform different functions are called homologous organs.

**Homology** in organs indicates common ancestry. It is based on **divergent evolution**, wherein a same basic organ in different organisms gets specialised to perform different functions, in order to adapt to the different environmental conditions prevailing in the habitat.

### Analogous Organs and Analogy

In contrast to homologous organs, the analogous organs are different in their anatomical structure and developmental origin, but appear same and perform similar functions. This relationship between the structures of different groups of animals due to their similar functions is called **analogy**. It is based on **convergent evolution** wherein similar habitats lead to the selection of similar features in different groups of organisms for the same function. .

## Requirements

Flash cards of homologous and analogous organs of plants and animals, pen and pencil.

## Procedure

1. Observe the flash cards and draw their respective figure.
2. Write the comments for each spot.

## Observations

1. **Homologous Organs in Plants**

   (i) **Thorns of *Bougainvillea* and tendrils of *Cucurbita*** Both of these structures, are the modifications of stem but they perform different functions. The thorns protects the plant from grazing animals, while tendrils provides support to the growing plant stem.

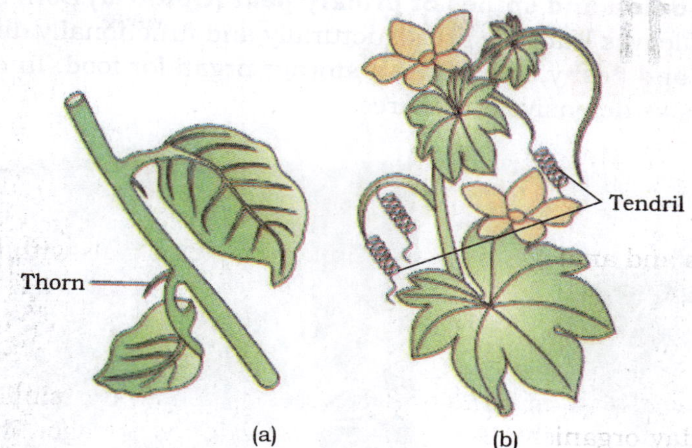


**Fig. 11.1** Homologous structure : (a) Thorn of *Bougainvillea* and (b) Tendril of *Cucurbita*

(ii) **Tendrils of *Vitis* and thorns of *Carissa*** Both of these structures originates from the terminal bud, but they are functionally different.

**Fig. 11.2** (a) Tendrils of *Vitis* (b) Thorns of *Carissa*

(iii) **Tendrils of balloon vine (*Cardiospermum*) and bulbils of *Agave*** Both of these structures are the modifications of floral bud, but they perform different functions. Tendrils help in climbing, whereas bulbils are involved in reproduction.

**Fig. 11.3** (a) Tendrils of baloon vine (b) Bulbils of *Agave*

(iv) **Scale leaves of onion and spines of prickly pear (*Opuntia*)** Both of these structures are modifications of leaves but they are structurally and functionally different. Scale leaves of onion are thick and fleshy, serving as a storage organ for food. In contrast, the spines of cactus functions as defensive structures.

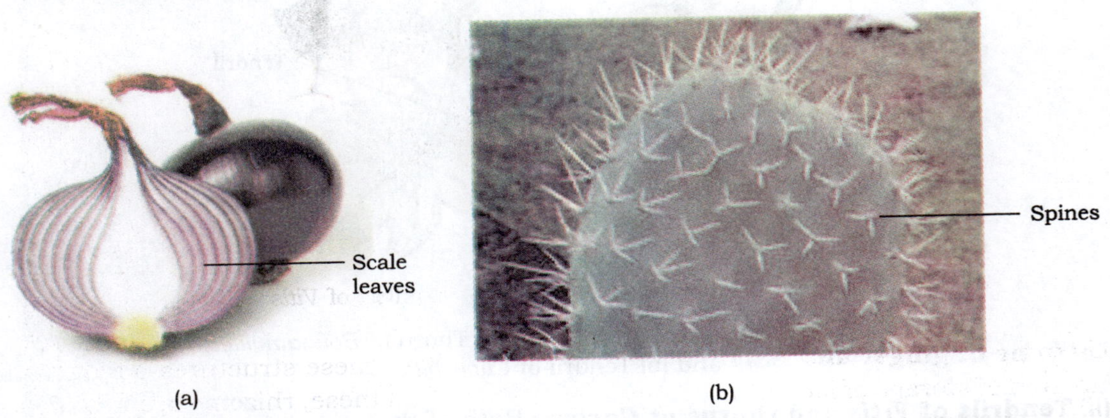


**Fig. 11.4** (a) Scale leaves of onion, (b) Spines of cactus

(v) **Tendrils of passion flower and thorns of pomegranate**

Both of these structures are structurally and functionally different but have similar origin i.e. they arise from axillary buds.

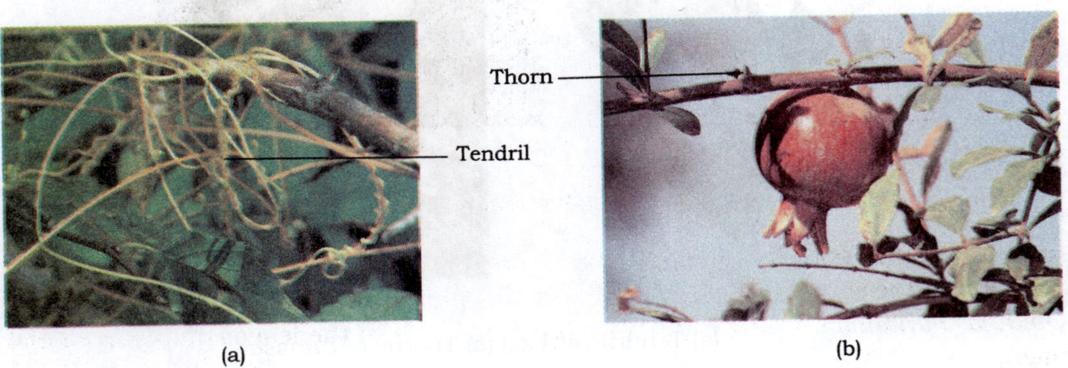


**Fig. 11.5** (a) Tendril of passion flower, (b) Thorn of pomegranate

2. **Analogous Organs in Plants**

(i) **Tendrils of pea and tendrils of *Vitis*** All tendrils are analogous with one another, being structurally and functionally similar, irrespective of their origin.

Tendrils of pea are the modification of leaf and in *Vitis* it is the modification of terminal bud.

(ii) **Thorns of pomegranate and spines of prickly pear** Both of them, thorns and spines are analogous structures being defensive in function. In these, thorns are the modifications of axillary buds, whereas spines are the modifications of leaves.

Fig. 11.6 (a) Tendrils of pea, (b) Tendrils of *Vitis*

(iii) **Rhizome of ginger and modified root of carrot** Both these structures perform similar function of storage of food but their origin is different. In these, rhizome is a modified stem where as carrot is a modified root.

Fig. 11.7 (a) Rhizome of ginger, (b) Modified root of carrot.

(iv) **Phylloclade, cladode and leaves** Phylloclade and cladode are both modification of stem that performs the same function as of leaves, i.e. photosynthesis. For example, phylloclade of *Opuntia, Parkinsonia* and *Asparagus* are analogous to the leaves of any local plant like mango.

Fig. 11.8 (a) Phylloclade of *Opuntia*, (b) Leaves of mango

3. **Homologous Organs in Animals**

(i) **Forelimbs of vertebrates** The basic structure of the forelimbs of almost all the vertebrates like human, cat, whale, bat , etc. are similar. All of them have the same bony elements (humerus, radio-ulna, carpals, metacarpals and phalanges), but perform different functions. For examples, human limbs are used for writing and grasping, whereas bats use their wings for flying and whales use their flippers for swimming, etc.

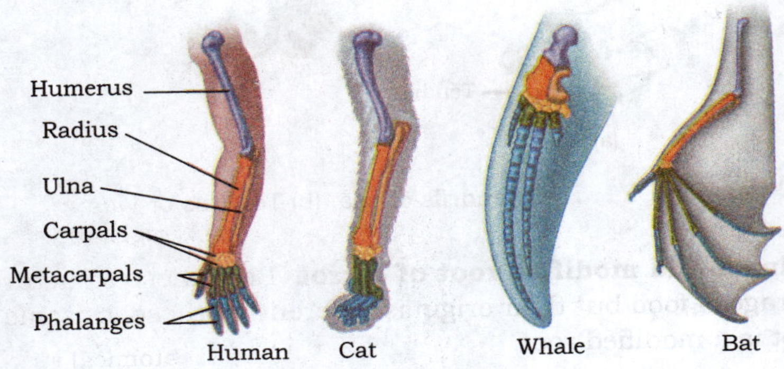


**Fig. 11.9** Homology of forelimbs in vertebrates

4. **Analogous Organs in Animals**

(i) **Wings of insects** and **birds** show analogy as both are well-adapted for flight. However, their basic structure is different as insects wings are formed from their integument (chitin), while the wings of birds are their modified forelimbs (feathers).

(ii) **Mandible of cockroach and mandible of vertebrates**

Both of these structures perform similar function but are different in origin.

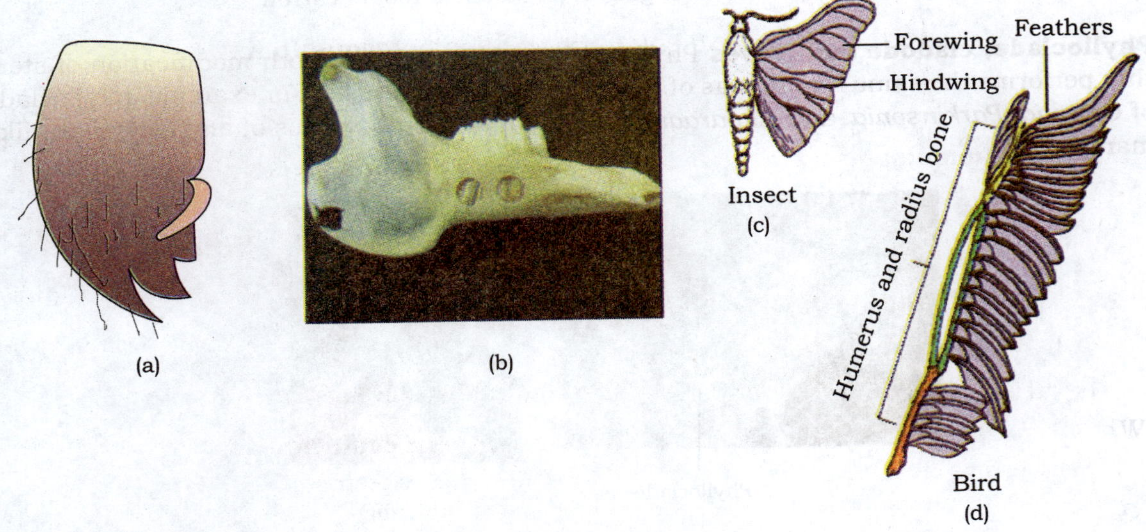


**Fig. 11.10** (a) Mandible of cockroach, (b) Mandible of rabbit, (c) Analogy in the wings of an insects and (d) a bird.

PRECAUTIONS

- The plant and animal flashcards should be handled carefully.
- Draw the diagrams carefully.

## Viva-Voce

**Q.1 What are homologous organs?**

**Ans** The organs found in different organisms which have a common origin and same basic structure, but differ in the functions are called homologous organs.

**Q.2 What are analogous organs?**

**Ans** The organs which have similar functions, but are different in anatomical structures and origins are called analogous organs.

**Q.3 What is the function of tendril?**

**Ans** Tendril provides support to the growing plant stem.

**Q.4 Write the analogous organs of cockroach and vertebrate.**

**Ans** Mandible of cockroach and mandible (lower jaw) of a vertebrate.

**Q.5 Write one homologous organ in plant.**

**Ans** Tendrils of *Vitis* and thorns of *Carissa*.

**Q.6 Write the analogous organs of insect and bird.**

**Ans** Wings of insect and wings of bird are analogous organs.

**Q.7 Name any two vertebrate's body parts that are homologous to human forelimbs (hands).**

**Ans** Flippers of whales and forelimbs of cheetah.

**Q.8 Select the homologous structures from the combinations given below:**

**(a) Forelimbs of whales and bats**

**(b) Tuber of potato and sweet potato**

**(c) Eyes of *Octopus* and mammals**

**(d) Thorns of *Bougainvillea* and tendrils of *Cucurbita*.**

**Ans** (a) and (d) represent the homologous structures. They exhibits divergent evolution.

**Q.9 Why are analogous structures a result of convergent evolution?**

**Ans** When organisms of different geographical location converge to a restricted habitat, they develop adaptations to suit that location and develop analogous structures.

**Q.10** **Why are stem and leaf tendrils considered as analogous organs?** NCERT

**Ans** Stem and leaf tendrils are considered as analogous structure because they have similar structure and function but have different origins.

**Q.11** **Suggest examples of homologous and analogous organs other than what are given in the manual.** NCERT

**Ans** Eye of an *Octopus* and a mammal are analogous organs mouth parts of cockroach and honey bee are homologous organs.

**Q.12** **Identify the examples of convergent evolution from the following.**

**(i) Flippers of penguins and dolphins.**

**(ii) Eyes of *Octopus* and mammals.**

**(iii) Vertebrate's brain.**

**Ans** (i) Flippers of penguins and dolphins.

(ii) Eyes of *Octopus* and mammals.

**Q.13** **What are vestigial organs and how they support the theory of evolution?**

**Ans** Vestigial organs are organs that have lost their function due to evolution. They support evolution because they imply that a creature has switched from utilising the structure to not using it or using it for a different purpose.

**Q.14** **Describe one example of adaptive radiation.**

**Ans** An example of adaptive radiation is Darwin's finches of the Galapagos Island, which once had a common ancestor, but with evolution, they modified into different types according to their food habits.

Experiment/Activity No.________ Date ________ Page No. ________

Teacher Signature ________________

Experiment/Activity No.________ Date ________ Page No. ________

Teacher Signature ________________

Experiment/Activity No.________ Date ________ Page No. ________

Teacher Signature ________

Experiment/Activity No.________ Date ________ Page No. ________

Teacher Signature ____________

Experiment/Activity No.________ Date ________ Page No. ________

Teacher Signature ________________

**Experiment/Activity No.**________ **Date** ________ **Page No.** ________

**Teacher Signature** ________________

Experiment/Activity No.________ Date ________ Page No. ________

Teacher Signature ________________

Experiment/Activity No.________ Date ________ Page No. ________

Teacher Signature ________

Experiment/Activity No.________ Date ________ Page No. ________

Teacher Signature ________

Experiment/Activity No.________ Date ________ Page No. ________

Teacher Signature________________

Experiment/Activity No.________ Date ________ Page No. ________

Teacher Signature ________

Experiment/Activity No.________ Date ________ Page No. ________

Teacher Signature ________________

Experiment/Activity No.________ Date ________ Page No. ________

Teacher Signature ________________

Experiment/Activity No.________ Date ________ Page No. ________

Teacher Signature ________________

Experiment/Activity No.________ Date ________ Page No. ________

Teacher Signature ________________

Experiment/Activity No.________ Date ________ Page No. ________

Teacher Signature ________________

Experiment/Activity No.________ Date ________ Page No. ________

Teacher Signature ________

Experiment/Activity No.________ Date ________ Page No. ________

Teacher Signature ________________

Experiment/Activity No.________ Date ________ Page No. ________

Teacher Signature ________

Experiment/Activity No.________ Date ________ Page No. ________

Teacher Signature ____________

Experiment/Activity No.________ Date ________ Page No. ________

Teacher Signature ________________

Experiment/Activity No.________ Date ________ Page No. ________

Teacher Signature ________________

Experiment/Activity No.________ Date ________ Page No. ________

Teacher Signature ____________

Experiment/Activity No.________ Date ________ Page No. ________

Teacher Signature ________________

Experiment/Activity No.________ Date ________ Page No. ________

Teacher Signature________

Experiment/Activity No.________ Date ________ Page No. ________

Teacher Signature ________________

Experiment/Activity No.________ Date ________ Page No. ________

Teacher Signature ________________

Experiment/Activity No.________ Date ________ Page No. ________

Teacher Signature ________________

Experiment/Activity No.________ Date ________ Page No. ________

Teacher Signature ________

Experiment/Activity No.________ Date ________ Page No. ________

Teacher Signature ________________

Experiment/Activity No.________ Date ________ Page No. ________

Teacher Signature ________

Experiment/Activity No.________ Date ________ Page No. ________

Teacher Signature ________________

Experiment/Activity No.________ Date ________ Page No. ________

Teacher Signature ________

Experiment/Activity No.________ Date ________ Page No. ________

Teacher Signature ________

Experiment/Activity No.________ Date ________ Page No. ________

Teacher Signature ________________

Experiment/Activity No.________ Date ________ Page No. ________

Teacher Signature ________________

Experiment/Activity No.________ Date ________ Page No. ________

Teacher Signature ________________

Experiment/Activity No.________ Date ________ Page No. ________

Teacher Signature ________

Experiment/Activity No.________ Date ________ Page No. ________

Teacher Signature ________________

Experiment/Activity No.________ Date ________ Page No. ________

Teacher Signature ________

Experiment/Activity No.________ Date ________ Page No. ________

Teacher Signature ________

Experiment/Activity No.________ Date ________ Page No. ________

Teacher Signature ________

Experiment/Activity No.________ Date ________ Page No. ________

Teacher Signature ________

Experiment/Activity No.________ Date ________ Page No. ________

Teacher Signature ________

Experiment/Activity No.________ Date ________ Page No. ________

Teacher Signature ________________

Experiment/Activity No.________ Date ________ Page No. ________

Teacher Signature ________

Experiment/Activity No.________ Date ________ Page No. ________

Teacher Signature ________

Experiment/Activity No.________ Date ________ Page No. ________

Teacher Signature ________

Experiment/Activity No.________ Date ________ Page No. ________

Teacher Signature ________________

Experiment/Activity No.________ Date ________ Page No. ________

Teacher Signature ________________

Experiment/Activity No.________ Date ________ Page No. ________

Teacher Signature ________________

Experiment/Activity No.________ Date ________ Page No. ________

Teacher Signature ________________

Experiment/Activity No.________ Date ________ Page No. ________

Teacher Signature ________

Experiment/Activity No.________ Date ________ Page No. ________

Teacher Signature ________________

Experiment/Activity No.________ Date ________ Page No. ________

Teacher Signature________________

Experiment/Activity No.________ Date ________ Page No. ________

Teacher Signature ________________

Experiment/Activity No.________ Date ________ Page No. ________

Teacher Signature ________________

Experiment/Activity No.________ Date ________ Page No. ________

Teacher Signature ________

Experiment/Activity No.________ Date ________ Page No. ________

Teacher Signature ________________

Experiment/Activity No.________ Date ________ Page No. ________

Teacher Signature ____________

Experiment/Activity No.________ Date ________ Page No. ________

Teacher Signature ________________

Experiment/Activity No.________ Date ________ Page No. ________

Teacher Signature ________

Experiment/Activity No.________ Date ________ Page No. ________

Teacher Signature ________________

Experiment/Activity No.________ Date ________ Page No. ________

Teacher Signature ________________

Experiment/Activity No.________ Date ________ Page No. ________

Teacher Signature ________________

Experiment/Activity No.________ Date ________ Page No. ________

Teacher Signature ________

Experiment/Activity No.________ Date ________ Page No. ________

Teacher Signature ________

Experiment/Activity No.________ Date ________ Page No. ________

Teacher Signature ________________

Experiment/Activity No.________ Date ________ Page No. ________

Teacher Signature ________________

Experiment/Activity No.________ Date ________ Page No. ________

Teacher Signature ________________

Experiment/Activity No.________ Date ________ Page No. ________

Teacher Signature ________________

Experiment/Activity No.________ Date ________ Page No. ________

Teacher Signature ________

Experiment/Activity No.________ Date ________ Page No. ________

Teacher Signature ________________

Experiment/Activity No.________ Date ________ Page No. ________

Teacher Signature ________

Experiment/Activity No.________ Date ________ Page No. ________

Teacher Signature ______________

Experiment/Activity No.________ Date ________ Page No. ________

Teacher Signature ________

Experiment/Activity No.________ Date ________ Page No. ________

Teacher Signature ________________

Experiment/Activity No.________ Date ________ Page No. ________

Teacher Signature________________

Experiment/Activity No.________ Date ________ Page No. ________

Teacher Signature ________________

Experiment/Activity No.________ Date ________ Page No. ________

Teacher Signature ________________